Appetizers and Beverages

Left: Indonesian Satay with Spicy Peanut Sauce
Right: Clockwise from top right, Pink, Slushy, Sparkling and Minted ReaLemonade (page 6)

INDONESIAN SATAY

¼ cup lime juice
2 cloves garlic, minced
1 teaspoon grated lime peel
½ teaspoon ground ginger
½ teaspoon ground red pepper
4 boneless skinless chicken breasts (about 2 pounds), cut into strips
Spicy Peanut Sauce (recipe follows)

Mix together lime juice, garlic, peel, ginger and pepper; pour over chicken. Cover. Refrigerate 1 hour. Drain.

Prepare coals for grilling.

Thread chicken on individual skewers; place on greased grill over hot coals (coals will be glowing).

Grill, uncovered, 3 to 5 minutes on each side or until tender. Serve with Spicy Peanut Sauce.

Makes 15 servings

SPICY PEANUT SAUCE

1 package (8 ounces) PHILADELPHIA BRAND® Cream Cheese, cubed
½ cup milk
3 tablespoons peanut butter
2 tablespoons brown sugar
½ teaspoon ground cardamom
⅛ teaspoon ground red pepper

- Stir ingredients in small saucepan over low heat until smooth.

Prep time: 20 minutes plus marinating
Cook time: 10 minutes

Nutrients per serving:

Calories	130	Cholesterol	35 mg
Fat	8 mg	Sodium	85 mg

Banana-Raspberry Smoothie

BANANA–RASPBERRY SMOOTHIE

2 ripe, medium DOLE® Bananas, peeled
1½ cups DOLE® Pure & Light Country Raspberry Juice, chilled
1 cup frozen vanilla yogurt, softened
1 cup DOLE® Fresh or frozen Raspberries

- Place all ingredients in blender. Process until smooth.

Makes 2 to 3 servings

Nutrients per serving:

Calories	196	Cholesterol	7 mg
Fat	2 g	Sodium	64 mg

REALEMONADE

½ cup sugar
½ cup REALEMON® Lemon Juice from Concentrate
3¼ cups cold water
Ice

In pitcher, dissolve sugar in ReaLemon® brand; add water. Cover; chill. Serve over ice.

Makes about 1 qua

Variations

Sparkling: Substitute club soda for cold water.

Slushy: Reduce water to ½ cup. In blender container, combine sugar, ReaLemon® brand and ½ cup water. Gradually add 4 cups ice cubes, blending until smooth. Serve immediately.

Pink: Stir in 1 to 2 teaspoons grenadine syrup or 1 to 2 drops red food coloring.

Minted: Stir in 2 to 3 drops peppermint extract.

Low Calorie: Omit sugar. Add 4 to 8 envelopes sugar substitute or 1½ teaspoons liquid sugar substitute.

Strawberry: Increase sugar to ¾ cup. In blender or food processor, purée 1 quart fresh strawberries, cleaned and hulled (about 1½ pounds): add to lemonade.

Grape: Stir in 1 (6-ounce) can frozen grape juice concentrate, thawed.

Nutrients per serving (1 cup):

Calories	97	Cholesterol	0 mg
Fat	trace	Sodium	6 mg

GROUND TURKEY CHINESE SPRING ROLLS

1 pound Ground Turkey
1 large clove garlic, minced
1½ teaspoons minced fresh ginger root
2 cups thinly sliced bok choy
½ cup thinly sliced green onions
2 tablespoons reduced-sodium soy sauce
1 teaspoon dry sherry or rice wine
1 teaspoon sesame oil
8 sheets phyllo pastry
Nonstick cooking spray

1. Preheat oven to 400°F.
2. In medium nonstick skillet, over medium-high heat, sauté turkey, garlic and ginger 4 to 5 minutes or until turkey is no longer pink. Drain thoroughly.
3. In medium bowl combine turkey mixture, bok choy, onions, soy sauce, sherry and oil.
4. On clean, dry counter, layer phyllo sheets into a stack and cut into 2 (18×7-inch) rectangles. Work with one rectangle of phyllo at a time. (Keep remaining phyllo covered with a damp cloth following package instructions.)
5. Coat rectangle of phyllo with nonstick cooking spray. On counter, arrange phyllo sheet so 7-inch side is parallel to counter edge. Place ¼ cup of turkey mixture in 5-inch strip, 1 inch away from bottom and side edges of phyllo. Fold 1-inch bottom edge of phyllo over filling and fold longer edges of phyllo toward center; roll up, jelly-roll style. Phyllo may break during rolling, but will hold filling once the roll is completed.
6. Repeat step 5 with remaining rectangles of phyllo to make remaining spring rolls. On 2 (10×15-inch) cookie sheets coated with nonstick cooking spray, place rolls, seam-side-down, and coat tops of rolls with nonstick cooking spray. Bake 14 to 16 minutes or until all surfaces of rolls are golden brown.
7. Serve immediately with Chinese mustard, hoisin sauce and additional soy sauce, if desired.

Makes 16 spring rolls

Nutrients per serving (1 spring roll):

Calories	86	Cholesterol	14 mg
Fat	3 g	Sodium	140 mg

Favorite recipe from **National Turkey Federation**

Ground Turkey Chinese Spring Rolls

TWELVE CARAT BLACK–EYED PEA RELISH

1 cup vinegar
¼ cup vegetable oil
2 cans (15 ounces each) black-eyed peas, drained
12 small carrots, steamed until crisp-tender, coarsely chopped
1 sweet onion, finely chopped
1 green bell pepper, finely chopped
1 cup sugar
¼ cup Worcestershire sauce
2 teaspoons black pepper
2 teaspoons salt (optional)
2 dashes ground red pepper

Combine vinegar and oil in small saucepan. Bring to a boil over high heat. Meanwhile, combine black-eyed peas, carrots, onion, green pepper, sugar, Worcestershire sauce, black pepper, salt and ground red pepper in large bowl. Pour oil mixture over vegetable mixture. Cover and refrigerate at least 24 hours to allow flavors to blend. Store, covered, in glass containers in refrigerator. Serve cold; garnish as desired.

Makes 2 to 3 pints

Nutrients per serving (⅓ cup):

Calories	112	Cholesterol	0 mg
Fat	3 g	Sodium	45 mg

Favorite recipe from the **Black-Eyed Pea Jamboree—Athens, Texas**

ARTICHOKE PUFFS

16 to 20 slices small party rye bread
2 tablespoons CRISCO® Shortening, melted
1 can (14 ounces) artichoke hearts, drained
2 egg whites
⅓ teaspoon salt
¼ cup grated Parmesan chee[se]
2 tablespoons shredded shar[p] Cheddar cheese
Dash ground red pepper
Paprika

1. Preheat oven to 400°F. Brush bre[ad] slices with melted Crisco® and place on an ungreased cookie shee[t].
2. Cut artichoke hearts in half; drain on paper towels. Place an artichok[e] piece, cut-side-down, on each bread slice.
3. Beat egg whites and salt until stiff not dry, peaks form. Fold in cheeses and ground red pepper.
4. Spoon about 1 measuring teaspoonful of egg white mixture over each artichoke piece; sprinkl[e] with paprika.
5. Bake at 400°F for 10 to 12 minut[es] or until golden brown. Serve hot. Garnish tray with celery leaves an[d] carrot curls, if desired.

Makes 16 pu[ffs]

Nutrients per serving (1 puff):

Calories	52	Cholesterol	2 m[g]
Fat	2 g	Sodium	113 m[g]

Twelve Carat Black-Eyed Pea Reli[sh]

Lite Delight

Introduction

MAKING SMART CHOICES

Everyone's concerned with calories, fat, cholesterol and sodium. Studies indicate that many Americans are overweight and that the American diet is loaded with too much fat and too many "empty calories"—calories from high-fat, high-sugar foods that supply few necessary nutrients. Other studies show a link between a poor diet and heart disease. As a result, Americans are waking up to the fact that a poor diet can lead to poor health.

The American Heart Association offers guidelines to help people adjust their diets to try to prevent heart and vascular diseases, and we've followed those guidelines in choosing the recipes for this magazine. The recipes that follow can help you make smart, healthy decisions about the foods you prepare. Every recipe is followed by a nutritional chart that tells you the number of calories, the grams (g) of fat, the milligrams (mg) of cholesterol and the milligrams (mg) of sodium for each serving of that recipe. Each recipe in this magazine has 300 calories or less per serving and contains 10 g or less of fat per serving. Mix and match your selection of recipes and foods so that your weekly diet follows guidelines for healthy eating.

Many of the recipes in this book are low-cholesterol and low-sodium as well. These recipes contain less than 50 mg of cholesterol and less than 300 mg of sodium. As you browse through, you'll see that most of the recipes fall well below these numbers.

The values of 300 calories, 10 g of fat, 50 mg cholesterol and 300 mg sodium per serving were chosen after careful consideration of a number of factors. The Food and Nutrition Board of the National Academy of Sciences proposes the Recommended Dietary Allowances (RDA) for essential nutrients, including calories, carbohydrates, fat, protein, amino acids, vitamins and minerals. The RDA were most recently revised in 1989. The RDA for calories are broken down according to age groups and sex. For healthy men between the ages of 19 and 50, for example, the RDA for total calorie intake are 2,900 calories per day. For healthy women between the ages of 19 and 50 (who are neither pregnant nor lactating), it is 2,200 calories per day. Thus, the 300 calories or less per serving for the recipes in this book represents only about 10 percent of the RDA for most men and about 14 percent of the RDA for most women.

The American Heart Association has recommended that total fat intake should be less than 30 percent of calories. For most women, that amounts to about 660 calories from fat or about 73 g of fat per day; for most men, that amounts to about 870 calories or about 97 g of fat. Thus the 10 g of fat or less per serving for each recipe in this book is well within recommended guidelines. The American Heart Association also recommends that cholesterol intake be less than 300 mg a day and that sodium intake not exceed 3,000 mg a day. In this book, low-cholesterol recipes recipes have 50 mg or less of cholesterol and low-sodium recipes have 300 mg or less of sodium.

ABOUT THE NUTRITIONAL INFORMATION

The analysis of each recipe includes all the ingredients that are listed in that recipe, except ingredients labeled as "optional" or "for garnish." If a range is given in the yield of a recipe ("Makes 6 to 8 servings," for example), the *higher* yield was used to calculate the per serving information. If a range is offered for an ingredient (¼ to ⅛ teaspoon, for example) the first amount given was used to calculate the nutrition information. If an ingredient is presented with an option ("2 tablespoons margarine or butter") the *first* item listed was used to calculate the nutrition information. Foods shown in photographs on the same serving plate and offered as "serve with" suggestions at the end of a recipe are also *not* included in the recipe analysis unless it is stated in the per serving line.

The nutrition information that appears with each recipe was submitted in part by the participating companies and associations. **Every effort has been made to check the accuracy of these numbers. However, because numerous variables account for a wide range of values for certain foods, all nutritive analyses that appear in this book should be considered approximate.** The numbers that appear in the nutrition charts are based on the nutritive values for foods in the U.S. Department of Agriculture Composition of Foods Handbook No. 8 (series), or from values submitted directly by the food manufacturers themselves.

ABOUT THE RECIPES

The recipes in this magazine were all selected to help you make smart choices about the foods you prepare. And with more than 120 recipes contributed by America's largest food companies, you'll find plenty to choose from. There are appetizers, beverages, soups and breads; meat, fish, poultry and pasta main dishes; salads, vegetable side dishes and desserts. From breakfast to dinner, from party fare to everyday meals, you can find wonderful, low-calorie, low-fat recipes to serve to family and friends.

This magazine offers you a wide variety of recipes that are, on a per serving basis, low in calories, fat and cholesterol. **The recipes in this book are NOT intended as a medically therapeutic program, nor as a substitute for medically approved diet plans for people on fat-, cholesterol- or sodium-restricted diets. You should consult your physician before beginning any diet plan.** The recipes offered here can be part of a healthy lifestyle that meets recognized dietary guidelines. A healthy lifestyle includes not only eating a balanced diet, but engaging in proper exercise as well.

Microwave cooking times in this book are approximate. Numerous variables, such as the microwave oven's rate wattage and the starting temperature, shape, amount and depth of the food, can affect cooking time. Use the cooking times as a guideline and check doneness before adding more time. Lower wattage ovens may consistently require longer cooking times.

So start on the road to better living and great eating with this marvelous collection of low-calorie, low-fat recipes.

CHEDDAR–RICE PATTIES

2 cups cooked rice
1 cup (4 ounces) shredded low-fat Cheddar cheese
½ cup minced onion
3 tablespoons all-purpose flour
½ teaspoon salt
¼ teaspoon ground black pepper
3 egg whites
⅛ teaspoon cream of tartar
Nonstick cooking spray
Apple wedges (optional)
Low-fat sour cream (optional)

Combine rice, cheese, onion, flour, salt, and pepper in medium bowl. Beat egg whites with cream of tartar in small bowl until stiff but not dry. Fold beaten egg whites into rice mixture.

Cheddar-Rice Patties

Coat large skillet with nonstick cooking spray and place over medium heat until hot. Spoon 2 to 3 tablespoons batter into skillet for each patty; push batter into diamond shape using spatula. Cook patties, turning once, until golden brown on both sides. Serve warm with apple wedges or sour cream.

Makes 4 servings, about 1 dozen

Nutrients per serving (3 patties):

Calories	233	Cholesterol	18 mg
Fat	6 g	Sodium	550 mg

Favorite recipe from **USA Rice Council**

MULLED CIDER

2 quarts apple cider
¾ to 1 cup REALEMON® Lemon Juice from Concentrate
1 cup firmly packed light brown sugar
8 whole cloves
2 cinnamon sticks
¾ cup rum (optional)
Additional cinnamon sticks for garnish (optional)

In large saucepan, combine all ingredients except rum and garnish; bring to a boil. Reduce heat; simmer, uncovered, 10 minutes to blend flavors. Remove spices; add rum just before serving, if desired. Serve hot with additional cinnamon sticks, if desired. *Makes about 2 quarts*

Tip: Can be served cold.

Nutrients per serving (¾ cup):

Calories	135	Cholesterol	0 mg
Fat	trace	Sodium	7 mg

APRICOT FRAPPÉ

2 cups apricot nectar
½ cup Light PHILADELPHIA BRAND® Pasteurized Process Cream Cheese Product
1 cup low-calorie ginger ale
3 tablespoons orange juice or orange-flavored liqueur
½ teaspoon vanilla
3 ice cubes

- Gradually add nectar to cream cheese product in blender or food processor container; cover. Blend until smooth.
- Add ginger ale, orange juice and vanilla; process until well blended. Add ice; process 1 minute. Garnish with fresh fruit, if desired.

Makes 6 servings

Prep time: 10 minutes

Nutrients per serving:

Calories	100	Cholesterol	10 mg
Fat	3 g	Sodium	120 mg

GARDEN VEGETABLE PLATTER

1 cup torn spinach
½ cup fresh parsley, stemmed
¼ cup cold water
3 tablespoons sliced green onions
½ teaspoon dried tarragon leaves, crushed
1 package (8 ounces) Light PHILADELPHIA BRAND® Neufchatel Cheese
¾ cup chopped cucumber
½ teaspoon lemon juice
3 drops hot pepper sauce
¼ teaspoon salt

Garden Vegetable Platter

- Bring to boil spinach, parsley, water, onions and tarragon in small saucepan. Reduce heat. Cover; simmer 1 minute. Drain.
- Place spinach mixture and all remaining ingredients in blender or food processor container; cover. Blend until smooth. Cover. Refrigerate. Serve with assorted vegetable dippers.

Makes 1½ cups

Prep time: 30 minutes plus refrigerating

Nutrients per serving (about 1 tablespoon):

Calories	25	Cholesterol	5 mg
Fat	2 g	Sodium	60 mg

TUNA–STUFFED ENDIVE

4 ounces soft-spread herb cheese
4 ounces reduced-calorie cream cheese, softened
1 teaspoon lemon or lime juice
2 heads Belgian endive or small lettuce leaves *or* crackers
1 can (3¼ ounces) STARKIST® Tuna, drained and finely flaked
Watercress sprigs or pimento strips for garnish

In blender container or food processor bowl, place cheeses and lemon juice. Cover and process until mixture is well blended. Trim ½ inch from bottom stems of endive; separate heads into leaves. Sprinkle 1 to 2 teaspoons tuna into each endive leaf; spoon or pipe 2 teaspoons of the cheese filling into each endive leaf. Garnish each with a sprig of watercress.

Makes about 24 appetizers

Nutrients per serving (1 appetizer):

Calories	29	Cholesterol	7 mg
Fat	2 g	Sodium	65 mg

PICKLE ROLL–EM–UPS

These delicious appetizers make attractive centerpieces on party platters or relish trays.

1 package (6 ounces) sliced ham
1 container (8 ounces) soft cream cheese
8 medium-sized CLAUSSEN® Whole Kosher Dill Pickles

Spread one side of each ham slice with one tablespoon cream cheese. Place one pickle on edge of each ham slice. Roll ham slice around pickle; press edges to seal. Cover and refrigerate one hour. To serve, cut each pickle into six slices.

Makes 48 appetizers

Nutrients per serving (1 appetizer):

Calories	20	Cholesterol	5 mg
Fat	2 g	Sodium	215 mg

PINEAPPLE–MELON COOLER

1 DOLE® Cantaloupe or favorite melon, cut into chunks
1 can (46 ounces) DOLE® Pineapple Juice
1 DOLE® Orange, juiced
Ice cubes
Pineapple chunks and whole strawberries for garnish

- Place melon in blender. Process until puréed; use 2 cups for recipe. Combine 2 cups puréed melon with pineapple juice and orange juice in large pitcher. Chill.
- Pour over ice in glasses. Garnish with pineapple and strawberry.

Makes 8 servings, 2 quarts

Nutrients per serving (1 cup):

Calories	126	Cholesterol	0 mg
Fat	trace	Sodium	6 mg

MEDITERRANEAN APPETIZER

1 container (8 ounces) Light PHILADELPHIA BRAND® Pasteurized Process Cream Cheese Product, softened
2 teaspoons red wine vinegar
1 clove garlic, minced
½ teaspoon dried oregano leaves, crushed
½ teaspoon lemon pepper
24 lahvosh crackers (3 inches in diameter) or 4 pita bread rounds, split
1½ cups finely torn spinach
1 tomato, chopped
4 ounces CHURNY® ATHENOS® Feta Cheese, crumbled
½ cup Greek ripe olives, pitted, chopped

- Stir cream cheese product, vinegar, garlic and seasonings in small bowl until well blended.
- Spread crackers with cream cheese mixture. Top with remaining ingredients. *Makes 8 servings*

Prep time: 20 minutes

Nutrients per serving:

Calories	180	Cholesterol	30 mg
Fat	10 g	Sodium	620 mg

Mediterranean Appetizer

Strawberry Watermelon Slush

SHRIMP CUCUMBER SPREAD

- **¼ cup MIRACLE WHIP® FREE® Nonfat Dressing**
- **2 ounces Light PHILADELPHIA BRAND® Neufchatel Cheese, softened**
- **¼ cup chopped cooked shrimp or flaked canned tuna**
- **3 tablespoons seeded chopped cucumber**
- **1 tablespoon green onion slices**
- **1 tablespoon chili sauce**

• Mix together ingredients until well blended; refrigerate. Serve with assorted crackers. *Makes 1 cup*

Prep time: 10 minutes plus refrigerating

Nutrients per serving (3 tablespoons):

Calories	60	Cholesterol	20 mg
Fat	3 g	Sodium	249 mg

STRAWBERRY WATERMELON SLUSH

- **1 pint fresh strawberries, cleaned and hulled (about ¾ pound)**
- **2 cups seeded and cubed watermelon**
- **⅓ cup sugar**
- **⅓ cup vodka (optional)**
- **¼ cup REALEMON® Lemon Juice from Concentrate**
- **2 cups ice cubes**

In blender container, combine all ingredients except ice; blend well. Gradually add ice, blending until smooth. Serve immediately. Garnish as desired. *Makes about 1 quart*

Nutrients per serving (1 cup):

Calories	110	Cholesterol	0 mg
Fat	1 g	Sodium	6 mg

CHERRY PUNCH

- **1 can (6 ounces) frozen lemonade concentrate, thawed**
- **5 cups DOLE® Pure & Light Mountain Cherry Juice, chilled**
- **1 bottle (28 ounces) mineral water, chilled**
- **DOLE® Lemon slices for garnish**
- **Mint sprigs for garnish**

• Reconstitute lemonade according to label directions in large punch bowl. Add remaining ingredients. *Makes 16 servings*

Nutrients per serving:

Calories	61	Cholesterol	0 mg
Fat	trace	Sodium	4 mg

GUACAMOLE WITH TORTILLA CHIPS

Guacamole and chips on a diet? You bet, when they are made with our tasty recipes.

1 package (4-serving size) JELL-O® Brand Lemon Flavor Sugar Free Gelatin
1 cup boiling water
1 container (16 ounces) 1% low-fat cottage cheese
1 cup chopped ripe avocado
¾ cup chopped scallions, divided
¼ cup drained pickled jalapeño slices
¼ cup lemon juice
2 cloves garlic
1 to 2 teaspoons chili powder
¼ cup diced tomato
4 sliced ripe olives
Chili Tortilla Chips (recipe follows)

- Completely dissolve gelatin in boiling water in small bowl. Pour into blender container. Add cottage cheese, avocado, ½ cup of scallions, jalapeños, lemon juice, garlic and chili powder. Blend on low speed, scraping down sides occasionally, about 2 minutes or until mixture is completely smooth. Pour into shallow 5-cup serving dish; smooth top. Chill until set, about 4 hours.
- Just before serving, garnish with remaining ¼ cup chopped scallions, tomato and ripe olives. Serve as a dip with fresh vegetables or Chili Tortilla Chips.

Makes 12 servings

Nutrients per serving:

Calories	60	Cholesterol	0 mg
Fat	3 g	Sodium	230 mg

CHILI TORTILLA CHIPS

These chips are lower in calories than regular tortilla chips because they are baked and not fried.

6 flour tortillas (7 inches in diameter)
Nonstick cooking spray
Chili powder

- Heat oven to 350°F. Lightly spray tortillas with nonstick cooking spray; sprinkle with chili powder. Turn tortillas over; repeat process. Cut into 8 pie-shaped wedges. Place on cookie sheet; bake 8 to 10 minutes until crisp and lightly browned.

Makes 12 servings

Nutrients per serving (4 chips):

Calories	60	Cholesterol	0 mg
Fat	1 g	Sodium	90 mg

Guacamole with Tortilla Chips

Breakfast and Brunch

Left: Rice Bran Buttermilk Pancakes
Right: Irish Soda Bacon Bread
(page 18)

RICE BRAN BUTTERMILK PANCAKES

1 cup rice flour or all-purpose flour
¾ cup rice bran
1 tablespoon sugar
1 teaspoon baking powder
½ teaspoon baking soda
1¼ cups low-fat buttermilk
3 egg whites, beaten
Nonstick cooking spray
Fresh fruit or reduced-calorie syrup (optional)

Sift together flour, bran, sugar, baking powder, and baking soda into large bowl. Combine buttermilk and egg whites in small bowl; add to flour mixture. Stir until smooth. Pour ¼ cup batter onto hot griddle coated with nonstick cooking spray. Cook over medium heat until bubbles form on top and underside is lightly browned. Turn to brown other side. Serve with fresh fruit or syrup.

Makes about 10 (4-inch) pancakes

Variation: For Cinnamon Pancakes, add 1 teaspoon ground cinnamon to dry ingredients.

Nutrients per serving (1 pancake):

Calories	99	Cholesterol	119 mg
Fat	2 g	Sodium	1 mg

Favorite recipe from **USA Rice Council**

Pineapple-Orange Sauce

PINEAPPLE–ORANGE SAUCE

Sensational served over waffles, fruit or frozen yogurt.

1 can (20 ounces) DOLE® Pineapple Chunks, undrained
Juice and zest from 1 DOLE® Orange
1 tablespoon cornstarch
1 tablespoon sugar
1 teaspoon ground ginger

- Combine pineapple, ½ cup orange juice and 1 teaspoon orange zest with remaining ingredients in saucepan. Cook and stir until sauce boils and thickens. Cool to room temperature.
- Use sauce over frozen yogurt, pancakes or waffles.

Makes 8 servings, about 2 cups

Nutrients per serving (about ¼ cup sauce):

Calories	64	Cholesterol	0 mg
Fat	trace	Sodium	1 mg

IRISH SODA BACON BREAD

4 cups all-purpose flour
3 tablespoons sugar
1½ tablespoons low-sodium baking powder
1 teaspoon baking soda
6 tablespoons unsalted margarine or butter, cold
1 cup golden raisins
6 slices ARMOUR® Lower Salt Bacon, cooked crisp and crumbled
2 eggs
1½ cups buttermilk

Preheat oven to 375°F. Combine flour, sugar, baking powder and baking soda in large bowl; cut in margarine until mixture resembles coarse crumbs. Stir in raisins and bacon. Beat eggs slightly in small bowl; reserve 1 tablespoon egg. Add buttermilk and remaining eggs to flour mixture; stir to make soft dough.

Turn out onto lightly floured surface; knead about 1 to 2 minutes, or until smooth. Shape dough into round loaf. Spray round 2-quart casserole dish with nonstick cooking spray; place dough in dish. With floured knife, cut a 4-inch cross about ¼ inch deep on top of loaf. Brush with reserved egg.

Bake about 55 to 65 minutes, or until wooden toothpick inserted into center comes out clean. (Cover loaf with foil during last 30 minutes of baking to prevent overbrowning.) Cool on wire rack 10 minutes; remove from dish. Serve with light cream cheese or honey butter, if desired.

Makes 12 to 15 servings

Nutrients per serving:

Calories	231	Cholesterol	40 mg
Fat	7 g	Sodium	130 mg

BREAKFAST IN A CUP

3 cups cooked rice
1 cup (4 ounces) shredded Cheddar cheese, divided
1 can (4 ounces) diced green chilies
1 jar (2 ounces) diced pimientos, drained
⅓ cup skim milk
2 eggs, beaten
½ teaspoon ground cumin
½ teaspoon salt
½ teaspoon ground black pepper
Nonstick cooking spray

Combine rice, ½ cup cheese, chilies, pimientos, milk, eggs, cumin, salt, and pepper in large bowl. Divide mixture evenly into 12 muffin cups coated with nonstick cooking spray. Sprinkle with remaining ½ cup cheese. Bake at 400°F for 15 minutes or until set. *Makes 12 servings*

Tip: Breakfast Cups may be stored in the freezer in freezer bags or tightly sealed containers. To reheat frozen Breakfast Cups, microwave each cup on HIGH 1 minute.

Nutrients per serving (1 cup):

Calories	123	Cholesterol	45 mg
Fat	4 g	Sodium	368 mg

Favorite recipe from **USA Rice Council**

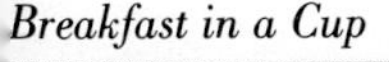

Breakfast in a Cup

Brunch Quesadillas with Fruit Salsa

BRUNCH QUESADILLAS WITH FRUIT SALSA

- **1 pint fresh strawberries, hulled and diced**
- **1 fresh ripe Anjou pear, cored and diced**
- **1 tablespoon chopped fresh cilantro**
- **1 tablespoon honey**
- **1 cup (4 ounces) SARGENTO® Preferred Light Fancy Shredded Mozzarella Cheese**
- **4 flour tortillas (8 inches in diameter)**
- **2 teaspoons light margarine, melted**
- **2 tablespoons light sour cream**

To make Fruit Salsa, combine strawberries, pear, cilantro and honey in medium bowl; set aside.

Sprinkle 2 tablespoons cheese on one half of each tortilla. Top with ⅓ cup salsa (drain and discard any liquid that has formed from the fruit) and another 2 tablespoons cheese on each tortilla. Fold tortillas in half. Brush top of each folded tortilla with some of the melted butter.

Grill folded tortillas, buttered-side-down, in dry preheated skillet until light golden brown and crisp, about 2 minutes. Brush tops with remaining melted butter; turn and brown other sides. Remove to serving plate or platter. Cut *each* tortilla in half. Serve with remaining Fruit Salsa. Garnish with sour cream. Serve immediately.

Makes 4 servings

Nutrients per serving:

Calories	278	Cholesterol	14 mg
Fat	9 g	Sodium	264 mg

BRAN–CHERRY BREAD

2 cups all-purpose flour
¾ cup sugar, divided
1 tablespoon baking powder
1 teaspoon salt
½ teaspoon ground nutmeg
1½ cups KELLOGG'S® CRACKLIN' OAT BRAN® Cereal
1¼ cups skim milk
1 egg
2 tablespoons vegetable oil
1 jar (10 ounces) maraschino cherries, drained and finely chopped
1 cup chopped walnuts, divided
1 tablespoon margarine

1. Combine flour, ½ cup sugar, baking powder, salt and nutmeg. Set aside.
2. In large mixing bowl, combine KELLOGG'S CRACKLIN' OAT BRAN Cereal and milk. Let stand 10 minutes or until cereal is softened. Add egg and oil. Beat well. Stir in flour mixture. Set aside 2 tablespoons chopped cherries. Fold remaining cherries and ¾ cup nuts into batter. Spread in 9×5×3-inch loaf pan coated with nonstick cooking spray.
3. Melt margarine in small skillet until bubbly. Remove from heat. Stir in remaining ¼ cup sugar, remaining ¼ cup nuts and reserved cherries. Sprinkle over batter.
4. Bake at 350°F about 1 hour. Cool in pan on wire rack 10 minutes. Remove from pan.

Makes 1 loaf, 15 slices

Nutrients per serving (1 slice):

Calories	240	Cholesterol	20 mg
Fat	9 g	Sodium	260 mg

CHEESE 'N' APPLE SPREAD

1 package (8 ounces) Light PHILADELPHIA BRAND® Neufchatel Cheese, softened
½ cup KRAFT® FREE® Nonfat Mayonnaise Dressing
½ cup (2 ounces) KRAFT® Light Naturals Shredded Mild Reduced Fat Cheddar Cheese
½ cup finely chopped apple

- Blend together neufchatel cheese and dressing. Stir in Cheddar cheese and apple; refrigerate. Serve on toasted bagelette halves.

Makes 1⅔ cups

Prep time: 10 minutes plus refrigerating

Nutrients per serving (2 tablespoons):

Calories	82	Cholesterol	5 mg
Fat	3 g	Sodium	420 mg

Bran-Cherry Bread

Raisin-Orange Muffins

RAISIN–ORANGE MUFFINS

1 cup whole wheat flour
½ cup uncooked rolled oats
¼ cup sugar
2 teaspoons baking powder
¼ teaspoon salt
¼ teaspoon ground allspice
⅔ cup skim milk
2 eggs, slightly beaten
2 tablespoons vegetable oil
1 teaspoon grated orange peel
¼ cup raisins

To Microwave: In large bowl, combine flour, oats, sugar, baking powder, salt and allspice. Make well in center. In small bowl, combine milk, eggs, oil and orange peel. Pour into flour mixture, stirring just until moistened. Batter will be lumpy. Fold in raisins.

Line 6 microwavable muffin pan cups with double paper liners. Spoon batter into each cup, filling half full. Microwave at HIGH 2 to 4½ minutes or until top springs back when touched. Rotate dish ½ turn halfway through cooking. Let stand 5 minutes. Remove from pan. Repeat procedure with remaining batter.

Makes 12 muffins

Nutrients per serving (1 muffin):

Calories	110	Cholesterol	36 mg
Fat	4 g	Sodium	118 mg

FIVE–MINUTE FRUIT DIP

½ cup MIRACLE WHIP® FREE® Nonfat Dressing
1 container (8 ounces) lemon-flavored low-fat yogurt

- Mix ingredients until well blended; refrigerate. Serve with assorted fruit kabobs. *Makes 1¼ cups*

Prep time: 5 minutes plus refrigerating

Nutrients per serving (2 tablespoons):

Calories	60	Cholesterol	0 mg
Fat	1 g	Sodium	230 mg

BREAKFAST SAUSAGE BAKE

2 tablespoons margarine
1 pound fresh mushrooms, finely chopped
1 cup dry fine bread crumbs
1 package (1 pound) LOUIS RICH® Turkey Breakfast Sausage, thawed
1 red or green pepper, chopped
3 tablespoons chopped fresh parsley *or* 1 tablespoon dried parsley flakes
¼ teaspoon ground red pepper
2 cartons (8 ounces each) cholesterol-free egg substitute *or* 8 eggs, beaten

- Preheat oven to 350°F. Melt margarine in large nonstick skillet oven medium-high heat. Add mushrooms. Cook and stir about 10 minutes or until mixture boils and moisture evaporates. Remove from heat; stir in bread crumbs.

- Spray 13×9-inch baking dish with nonstick cooking spray. Press mushroom mixture onto bottom of prepared baking dish to form crust.
- In same nonstick skillet, cook sausage over medium heat about 12 minutes, breaking sausage apart into small pieces and stirring frequently until lightly browned. Remove from heat.
- Stir in chopped red pepper, parsley and ground red pepper. Spread sausage mixture over crust; pour egg substitute evenly over mixture. Bake 25 to 30 minutes or until mixture is set. *Makes 12 servings*

Note: For 6 servings, use half of the ingredients; prepare and bake as above in 9-inch pie plate.

Nutrients per serving:

Calories	140	Cholesterol	20 mg
Fat	6 g	Sodium	370 mg

RAINBOW TROUT BREAKFAST FILLETS

½ cup all-purpose flour
1½ teaspoons paprika
1 teaspoon ground thyme
¼ teaspoon salt
Dash pepper
1 egg, beaten
4 CLEAR SPRINGS® Brand Idaho Rainbow Trout fillets (4 ounces each)
1 tablespoon olive oil

Combine flour, paprika, thyme, salt and pepper on waxed paper; set aside. Dip each trout fillet in egg; coat with seasoned flour mixture. Sauté trout in oil in large skillet over medium-high heat 1 to 2 minutes per side or until fish flakes easily with fork. Serve with fruit and garnish as desired.
Makes 4 servings

Nutrients per serving:

Calories	240	Cholesterol	115 mg
Fat	9 g	Sodium	179 mg

Rainbow Trout Breakfast Fillets

Top: Cheese Danish
Bottom: Belgian Waffle Dessert
(page 25)

CHEESE DANISH

You might be surprised to learn that a flour tortilla forms the shell for these inspired pastries. We've decorated the serving plate with a few fresh raspberries and a couple of sprigs of mint.

1 tablespoon sugar
1 teaspoon ground cinnamon
5 flour tortillas (6 or 7 inches in diameter)
Nonstick cooking spray
1 cup cold skim milk
1 package (4-serving size) JELL-O® Vanilla Flavor Sugar Free Instant Pudding and Pie Filling
1 container (8 ounces) light pasteurized process cream cheese product
2 cups thawed COOL WHIP® LITE® Whipped Topping
1 square BAKER'S® Semi-Sweet Chocolate

- Heat oven to 350°F.
- Mix sugar and cinnamon. Spray tortillas with nonstick cooking spray. Sprinkle each tortilla with scant ½ teaspoon sugar-cinnamon mixture. Turn tortillas over; repeat process. Cut each tortilla into 4 wedges. Stand rounded edge of each tortilla wedge in bottom of muffin cup by curling in sides. Bake 10 minutes or until lightly browned and crispy. Cool.
- Pour milk into large mixing bowl. Add pudding mix. Beat at low speed with electric mixer until well blended, 1 to 2 minutes. Beat in cream cheese product at medium speed until smooth. Gently stir in whipped topping. Refrigerate at least 1 hour.
- To serve, fill each tortilla shell with scant 3 tablespoons cheese mixture using pastry bag or spoon. Place chocolate in small plastic sandwich bag or self-closing bag. Microwave on HIGH about 1 minute or until chocolate is melted. Fold top of bag tightly; snip off one corner (about ⅛ inch). Hold bag tightly at top; drizzle chocolate through opening over prepared Danish. Refrigerate until chocolate sets, about 5 minutes.

Makes 20 Danish

Note: Freeze any leftover Danish. Thaw in refrigerator as needed.

Nutrients per serving (1 Danish):

Calories	90	Cholesterol	5 mg
Fat	4 g	Sodium	180 mg

BELGIAN WAFFLE DESSERT

An excellent choice for a brunch dessert. The berries provide an added bonus of 2 grams of fiber per serving.

2¼ cups cold 2% low-fat milk
2 tablespoons lemon juice
1 teaspoon grated lemon peel
1 package (4-serving size) JELL-O® Vanilla Flavor Sugar Free Instant Pudding and Pie Filling
1 cup thawed COOL WHIP® LITE® Whipped Topping
1 pint (about 2 cups) strawberries, quartered
½ pint (about 1 cup) raspberries
½ pint (about 1 cup) blueberries or blackberries
10 small frozen Belgian or regular waffles, toasted

- Pour milk, lemon juice and lemon peel into large mixing bowl. Add pudding mix. Beat with wire whisk until well blended, 1 to 2 minutes. Gently stir in whipped topping. Refrigerate.
- Mix fruit in bowl; refrigerate.
- To serve, spoon about 3 tablespoons pudding mixture on each dessert plate. Top each with waffle, additional 2 tablespoons pudding mixture and scant ½ cup fruit. Assemble desserts as needed. Store leftover pudding mixture and fruit in refrigerator. *Makes 10 waffles*

Nutrients per serving (1 waffle):

Calories	170	Cholesterol	5 mg
Fat	5 g	Sodium	310 mg

GINGERBREAD PANCAKES

1½ cups all-purpose flour
½ cup SPOON SIZE® Shredded Wheat, finely rolled (about ⅓ cup crumbs)
1 tablespoon DAVIS® Baking Powder
1 teaspoon pumpkin pie spice
1¼ cups skim milk
½ cup EGG BEATERS® 99% Real Egg Product
3 tablespoons BRER RABBIT® Light Molasses
2 tablespoons FLEISCHMANN'S® Margarine, melted

In large bowl, mix flour, cereal, baking powder and pumpkin pie spice. In small bowl, blend milk, egg product, molasses and margarine; stir into dry ingredients just until moistened.

On lightly greased preheated griddle or skillet, pour ¼ cup batter for each pancake. Cook over medium heat until surface is bubbly and bottom is lightly browned. Turn carefully and cook until done. Remove and keep warm.
Makes 12 pancakes

Nutrients per serving (1 pancake):

Calories	110	Cholesterol	1 mg
Fat	2 g	Sodium	128 mg

BREAKFAST BURRITO

4 slices LOUIS RICH® Turkey Bacon
2 flour tortillas (7 inches in diameter)
2 tablespoons shredded sharp Cheddar cheese
2 large egg whites
1 tablespoon chopped mild chilies
Salsa or taco sauce (optional)
Additional shredded sharp Cheddar cheese (optional)

- Cook turkey bacon in nonstick skillet over medium-high heat 8 to 10 minutes or until lightly browned.
- Place 2 turkey bacon slices on each tortilla; sprinkle each with 1 tablespoon cheese.
- Beat egg whites and chilies; add to hot skillet. Cook and stir about 2 minutes or until set.
- Divide egg mixture between tortillas. Fold tortillas over filling. Top with salsa and additional cheese, if desired. *Makes 2 burritos*

To keep burritos warm: Wrap filled burritos in foil and place in warm oven up to 30 minutes.

Nutrients per serving (1 burrito):

Calories	220	Cholesterol	25 mg
Fat	9 g	Sodium	470 mg

Breakfast Burrito

COUNTRY BREAKFAST CEREAL

3 cups cooked brown rice
2 cups skim milk
½ cup raisins or chopped prunes
1 tablespoon margarine (optional)
1 teaspoon ground cinnamon
⅛ teaspoon salt
Honey or brown sugar (optional)
Fresh fruit (optional)

Combine rice, milk, raisins, margarine, cinnamon, and salt in 2- to 3-quart saucepan. Bring to a boil; stir once or twice. Reduce heat to medium-low; cover and simmer 8 to 10 minutes or until thickened. Serve with honey and fresh fruit.

Makes 6 servings

Nutrients per serving:

Calories	174	Cholesterol	2 mg
Fat	1 g	Sodium	98 mg

Favorite recipe from **USA Rice Council**

Peachy Cinnamon Coffee Cake

PEACHY CINNAMON COFFEE CAKE

1 package DUNCAN HINES® Bakery Style Cinnamon Swirl with Crumb Topping Muffin Mix
1 can (8¼ ounces) juice pack sliced yellow cling peaches
Water
1 egg

1. Preheat oven to 400°F. Grease 8-inch square or 9-inch round pan.
2. Drain peaches, reserving juice. Add water to reserved juice to equal ¾ cup liquid. Chop peaches.
3. Combine muffin mix, egg and ¾ cup peach liquid in medium bowl; fold in peaches. Pour batter into pan. Knead swirl packet 10 seconds before opening. Squeeze contents on top of batter and swirl with knife. Sprinkle topping over batter.
4. Bake at 400°F for 28 to 33 minutes for 8-inch pan (or 20 to 25 minutes for 9-inch pan) or until golden. Serve warm.

Makes 9 servings

Nutrients per serving:

Calories	205	Cholesterol	0 mg
Fat	7 g	Sodium	248 mg

Soups and Breads

Left: Golden Tomato Soup
Right: Onion Flatbread (page 30)

GOLDEN TOMATO SOUP

4 teaspoons reduced-calorie margarine
1 cup chopped onion
2 cloves garlic, coarsely chopped
½ cup chopped carrot
¼ cup chopped celery
8 medium tomatoes, blanched, peeled, seeded, chopped
6 cups chicken broth
2 tablespoons uncooked rice
2 tablespoons tomato paste
1 tablespoon Worcestershire sauce
¼ to ½ teaspoon pepper
½ teaspoon dried thyme
5 drops hot pepper sauce

Melt margarine in large Dutch oven over medium-high heat. Add onion and garlic; cook and stir 1 to 2 minutes or until tender. Add carrot and celery; cook 7 to 9 minutes or until tender, stirring frequently. Stir in tomatoes, broth, rice, tomato paste, Worcestershire sauce, pepper, thyme and hot pepper sauce. Reduce heat to low; cook about 30 minutes, stirring frequently.

Remove from heat. Let cool about 10 minutes. In food processor or blender, process soup in small batches until smooth. Return soup to Dutch oven; simmer 3 to 5 minutes or until heated through. Garnish as desired.

Makes 8 servings

Nutrients per serving:

Calories	91	Cholesterol	1 mg
Fat	2 g	Sodium	641 mg

Favorite recipe from **Florida Tomato Committee**

ONION FLATBREAD

2⅓ cups warm water (105° to 115°F), divided
½ cup plus 3 tablespoons honey, divided
1½ packages dry yeast
6 tablespoons olive oil, divided
3 cups whole wheat flour
⅓ cup cornmeal
2 tablespoons coarse salt
3 to 4 cups all-purpose flour, divided
2 large red onions, thinly sliced
1 cup red wine vinegar
Additional cornmeal
1 cup grated Parmesan cheese
Freshly ground pepper to taste

Combine ⅓ cup water and 3 tablespoons honey in large bowl; sprinkle yeast over water. Let stand about 15 minutes until bubbly. Add remaining 2 cups water, 3 tablespoons olive oil, whole wheat flour and cornmeal. Mix until well blended. Stir in salt and 2 cups all-purpose flour. Gradually stir in enough remaining flour until mixture clings to sides of bowl.

Turn out onto lightly floured surface. Knead in enough remaining flour to make a smooth and satiny dough, about 10 minutes. Divide dough in half. Place each half in large, lightly greased bowl; turn over to grease surface. Cover; let rise in warm place (85°F) until doubled.

Meanwhile, combine onions, vinegar and remaining ½ cup honey. Marinate at least 1 hour.

Grease 2 (12-inch) pizza pans and sprinkle with additional cornmeal. Stretch and pat out dough on prepared pizza pans; create valleys with fingertips. Cover; let dough rise in warm place (85°F) until doubled, about 1 hour. Drain onions; scatter them over dough. Sprinkle with remaining 3 tablespoons olive oil and Parmesan cheese; season with pepper.

Makes 2 flatbreads, 16 servings

Nutrients per serving (1 wedge):

Calories	296	Cholesterol	5 mg
Fat	8 g	Sodium	916 mg

Favorite recipe from ***The Times-Picayune***

THREE-BEAN CHILI

1 can (16 ounces) tomatoes, cut into bite-size pieces
1 jar (12 ounces) HEINZ® HomeStyle Brown Gravy
1 tablespoon chili powder
1 can (15 ounces) chili beans in chili gravy
1 can (15 ounces) garbanzo beans, drained
1 can (15 ounces) pinto or kidney beans, drained
1 can (4 ounces) chopped green chilies
Plain nonfat yogurt or light dairy sour cream, sliced green onions and/or shredded low-fat Cheddar cheese

Combine tomatoes, gravy and chili powder in 3-quart saucepan. Bring to a boil over high heat. Stir in beans and chilies. Reduce heat to low. Cover; simmer 15 minutes, stirring occasionally. Serve with desired toppings.

Makes 6 servings, about 6½ cups

Nutrients per serving (about 1 cup):

Calories	281	Cholesterol	0 mg
Fat	4 g	Sodium	1135 mg

Basil-Vegetable Soup

BASIL–VEGETABLE SOUP

1 package (9 ounces) frozen cut green beans
1 can (15 ounces) cooked cannellini beans, undrained
3 medium carrots, cut into thin slices
3 medium zucchini or yellow squash, cut into thin slices
2 quarts beef broth
2 cloves garlic, minced
Salt and pepper to taste
2 to 3 ounces uncooked vermicelli or spaghetti
½ cup tightly packed fresh basil leaves, finely chopped
Grated Romano cheese

Combine beans, carrots, zucchini, broth and garlic in Dutch oven. Bring to a boil over high heat. Reduce heat to low. Cover; simmer until carrots are tender. Season to taste with salt and pepper. Add vermicelli; bring to a boil over high heat. Reduce heat to low. Simmer until pasta is tender, yet firm. (If desired, pasta may be cooked separately, then added to soup just before serving.) Add basil; continue to simmer until basil is completely tender. Sprinkle with cheese.

Makes 10 to 12 servings

Nutrients per serving:

Calories	110	Cholesterol	trace
Fat	1 g	Sodium	585 mg

WILD RICE SOUP

⅓ cup chopped carrot
⅓ cup chopped celery
⅓ cup chopped onion
2 teaspoons margarine or butter
1⅓ cups cooked wild rice
1 jar (12 ounces) HEINZ® HomeStyle Turkey Gravy
1½ cups skim milk
2 tablespoons dry sherry

Sauté vegetables in margarine in 2-quart saucepan over medium-high heat until tender. Stir in rice, gravy and milk. Reduce heat to low. Simmer 5 minutes. Stir in sherry.

Makes 4 servings, about 4 cups

Nutrients per serving (about 1 cup):

Calories	164	Cholesterol	7 mg
Fat	4 g	Sodium	645 mg

Meatball & Vegetable Soup

MEATBALL & VEGETABLE SOUP

1 pound lean ground beef
½ cup fresh bread crumbs (1 slice)
⅓ cup chopped onion
1 egg, slightly beaten
4 teaspoons WYLERS® or STEERO® Beef-Flavor Instant Bouillon
⅛ teaspoon garlic powder
6 cups water
1 (28-ounce) can whole tomatoes, undrained and broken up
½ teaspoon pepper
2 cups frozen hash brown potatoes
1 cup frozen peas and carrots

In bowl, combine meat, crumbs, onion, egg, 1 teaspoon bouillon and garlic powder; mix well. Shape into 1-inch meatballs. In Dutch oven, brown meatballs; pour off fat. Add water, tomatoes, pepper and remaining 3 teaspoons bouillon. Bring to a boil; reduce heat. Simmer, uncovered, 20 minutes. Stir in vegetables; cook 15 minutes or until tender, stirring occasionally. Refrigerate leftovers.
Makes about 2½ quarts

Nutrients per serving:

Calories	201	Cholesterol	49 mg
Fat	10 g	Sodium	378 mg

HEARTY MINESTRONE GRATINÉ

1 cup diced zucchini
1 cup diced celery
1 can (28 ounces) tomatoes, chopped, liquid reserved
2 cups water
2 teaspoons sugar
1 teaspoon dried Italian herb seasoning
1 can (15 ounces) garbanzo beans, drained
4 slices French bread (each 3×½ inches), toasted
1 cup (4 ounces) SARGENTO® Preferred Light Fancy Shredded Mozzarella Cheese
2 tablespoons SARGENTO® Grated Parmesan Cheese
Freshly chopped parsley

Spray large saucepan or Dutch oven with nonstick cooking spray. Over medium heat, sauté zucchini and celery until tender. Add tomatoes, water, sugar and herb seasoning. Simmer, uncovered, 15 to 20 minutes. Add garbanzo beans; simmer 10 minutes.

Meanwhile, heat broiler. Place toasted bread on broiler pan. Divide mozzarella evenly over bread slices. Broil until cheese melts. Ladle soup into bowls and top with cheese-topped bread slices. Sprinkle Parmesan cheese over bread slices and garnish with parsley. Serve immediately.
Makes 4 servings

Nutrients per serving:

Calories	273	Cholesterol	15 mg
Fat	5 g	Sodium	999 mg

PICANTE ONION SOUP

3 cups thinly sliced onions
1 clove garlic, minced
¼ cup butter or margarine
2 cups tomato juice
1 can (10½ ounces) condensed beef broth
1 soup can water
½ cup PACE® Picante Sauce
1 cup unseasoned croutons (optional)
1 cup (4 ounces) shredded Monterey Jack cheese (optional)
Additional PACE® Picante Sauce

Cook onions and garlic in butter in 3-quart saucepan over medium-low heat about 20 minutes, stirring frequently, until onions are tender and golden brown. Stir in tomato juice, broth, water and ½ cup picante sauce; bring to a boil over high heat.

Picante Onion Soup

Reduce heat to low. Simmer, uncovered, 20 minutes. Ladle soup into bowls and sprinkle with croutons and cheese. Serve with additional picante sauce. *Makes 6 servings*

Nutrients per serving:

Calories	119	Cholesterol	trace
Fat	8 g	Sodium	1051 mg

CHEDDAR–ONION CASSEROLE BREAD

2½ cups flour
1 tablespoon baking powder
½ teaspoon salt
½ cup HELLMANN'S® or BEST FOODS® Light Reduced Calorie Mayonnaise
2 cups (8 ounces) shredded Cheddar cheese
½ cup minced green onions
¾ cup milk
1 egg

Preheat oven to 425°F. Grease 1½-quart casserole. In large bowl, combine flour, baking powder and salt. Stir in mayonnaise until mixture resembles coarse crumbs. Add cheese and green onions; toss. In small bowl, beat milk and egg. Stir into cheese mixture just until moistened. Spoon into prepared casserole.

Bake 35 to 45 minutes or until toothpick inserted into center comes out clean. Cut into wedges; serve immediately.

Makes 1 loaf, 12 wedges

Nutrients per serving (1 wedge):

Calories	214	Cholesterol	43 mg
Fat	10 g	Sodium	301 mg

CRUSTY OVAL ROLLS

1 package active dry yeast
1⅓ cups warm water (105° to 115°F)
1 tablespoon honey
1 tablespoon shortening, melted, cooled
1 teaspoon salt
3¼ to 4 cups bread flour
¼ cup cold water
1 teaspoon cornstarch

In large bowl, combine yeast and warm water; stir to dissolve yeast. Stir in honey, shortening, salt and 2½ cups flour; beat until very elastic. Stir in enough remaining flour to make dough easy to handle.

Turn out onto floured surface. Knead 15 minutes or until dough is smooth and elastic, adding as much remaining flour as needed to prevent sticking. Shape dough into ball. Place in large, greased bowl; turn dough once to grease surface. Cover with towel; let rise in warm place (85°F) until doubled, about 1 hour.

Punch dough down; knead briefly on floured surface. Cover; let rest 10 minutes. Divide dough into 10 equal pieces; shape each piece into ball. Starting at center and working toward opposite ends, roll each ball on floured surface with palms of hands into tapered oval. Place, evenly spaced, on 2 greased baking sheets. Cover; let rise in warm place until almost doubled, about 25 minutes.

In small saucepan, combine cold water and cornstarch. Bring to a boil over high heat, stirring constantly. Boil until thickened and clear, about 2 minutes; cool slightly. Brush risen rolls with warm cornstarch mixture. Slash each roll lengthwise with sharp knife about ½ inch deep and about ½ inch from each end.

Preheat oven to 375°F. Bake 30 to 35 minutes or until rolls are golden brown and sound hollow when tapped. Remove to wire racks to cool.

Makes 10 rolls

Nutrients per serving (1 roll):

Calories	180	Cholesterol	0 mg
Fat	2 g	Sodium	214 mg

Crusty Oval Rolls

NAVY BEAN SOUP

2 tablespoons vegetable oil
1 cup chopped leeks
1½ cups (6 ounces) ARMOUR® Lower Salt Ham cut into ½-inch cubes
1 cup uncooked navy beans, soaked overnight and drained
1 tablespoon chopped jalapeño peppers

Heat oil in 3-quart saucepan over medium heat. Add leeks; sauté 3 to 5 minutes or until tender. Stir in ham, beans and peppers; add enough water to just cover beans. Bring to a boil over high heat. Reduce heat to low. Cover; simmer 1 to 1½ hours or until beans are tender.

Makes 4 servings

Nutrients per serving:

Calories	282	Cholesterol	21 mg
Fat	10 g	Sodium	420 mg

BEEF NOODLE SOUP

2 tablespoons CRISCO® PURITAN® Oil
½ pound boneless beef sirloin, cut into thin strips
¼ cup chopped green onion
1 tablespoon all-purpose flour
3 cans (10½ ounces each) condensed chicken broth
3 cups water
2 cups cooked vermicelli or very fine egg noodles

1. Heat Crisco® Puritan® Oil in 3-quart saucepan. Add beef. Cook over medium-high heat until beef is browned.

2. Add onion. Cook, stirring occasionally, about 2 minutes, or until onion is tender. Stir in flour. Add chicken broth and water.

3. Heat to boiling, stirring occasionally. Reduce heat to low. Simmer about 5 minutes. Stir in noodles. Simmer until soup is heated through.

Makes 10 servings

Nutrients per serving:

Calories	144	Cholesterol	28 mg
Fat	6 g	Sodium	579 mg

POTATO–CHEESE CALICO SOUP

1 pound potatoes, peeled and thinly sliced
1 cup sliced onion
2½ cups chicken broth
½ cup low-fat milk
1 cup sliced mushrooms
½ cup diced red bell pepper
½ cup sliced green onions
1 cup (4 ounces) finely shredded Wisconsin Asiago Cheese
Salt and black pepper
2 tablespoons chopped parsley

In 3-quart saucepan, combine potatoes, 1 cup onion and broth. Bring to boil. Reduce heat to low. Cover; cook until potatoes are tender, about 10 minutes. Pour into blender container; blend until smooth. Return to saucepan. Stir in milk, mushrooms, bell pepper and green onions. Bring to simmer over medium-low heat. Add cheese, a few tablespoons at a time, stirring to melt. Season with salt and black pepper. Sprinkle with parsley.

Makes 6 servings, 6 cups

Nutrients per serving (1 cup):

Calories	151	Cholesterol	9 mg
Fat	4 g	Sodium	526 mg

Favorite recipe from **Wisconsin Milk Marketing Board**

OAT–RAISIN BREAD

Made with whole wheat flour, oats and raisins, this healthful bread is a good source of fiber.

1½ cups all-purpose flour
1 cup whole wheat flour
1 cup uncooked quick or old-fashioned oats
2 teaspoons baking soda
½ teaspoon salt
2 eggs
1½ cups buttermilk
½ cup KARO® Light or Dark Corn Syrup
½ cup packed brown sugar
¼ cup MAZOLA® Corn Oil
1 cup raisins

Preheat oven to 350°F. Grease and flour two 9×5×3-inch loaf pans. In large bowl, combine flours, oats, baking soda and salt. In small bowl, combine eggs, buttermilk, corn syrup, brown sugar and corn oil until blended. Stir into flour mixture just until moistened. Stir in raisins. Pour batter into prepared pans.

Bake 45 to 50 minutes or until wooden toothpick inserted into centers comes out clean. Cool in pans on wire racks 10 minutes. Remove from pans; cool on wire rack.

Makes 2 loaves, 24 slices

Prep time: 15 minutes
Bake time: 50 minutes plus cooling

Nutrients per serving (1 slice):

Calories	158	Cholesterol	18 mg
Fat	3 g	Sodium	142 mg

CLAM CHOWDER

3 tablespoons CRISCO® Shortening
2 large yellow onions, peeled and thinly sliced
6 medium potatoes (about 2 pounds), pared and thinly sliced
1½ cups water
2 cans (10 ounces each) shelled whole baby clams *or* 3 cans (6½ ounces each) minced clams, undrained
1 quart milk
1 teaspoon salt
¼ teaspoon ground white pepper

1. Melt Crisco® in large, heavy saucepan. Sauté onions and potatoes for about 5 minutes until golden brown. Add water; heat to boiling. Reduce heat; simmer, covered, 10 to 15 minutes or until potatoes are tender. Stir in clams and their liquid. Heat 2 to 3 minutes. Remove from heat. Add milk, salt and pepper.
2. Cool mixture, uncovered, 30 minutes, then set, uncovered, in the refrigerator. About 20 minutes before serving, heat chowder over medium-low heat just until steam rises from top (about 20 minutes); *do not boil.*

Makes 12 servings, 3 quarts

Nutrients per serving (1 cup):

Calories	180	Cholesterol	23 mg
Fat	5 g	Sodium	295 mg

HEARTY CHICKEN AND RICE SOUP

10 cups chicken broth
1 medium onion, chopped
1 cup sliced celery
1 cup sliced carrots
¼ cup snipped parsley
½ teaspoon cracked black pepper
½ teaspoon dried thyme leaves
1 bay leaf
1½ cups chicken cubes (about ¾ pound)
2 cups cooked rice
2 tablespoons lime juice
Lime slices for garnish

Combine broth, onion, celery, carrots, parsley, pepper, thyme, and bay leaf in Dutch oven. Bring to a boil over high heat. Stir once or twice. Reduce heat to low. Simmer, uncovered, 10 to 15 minutes. Add chicken; simmer, uncovered, 5 to 10 minutes or until chicken is cooked. Remove and discard bay leaf. Stir in rice and lime juice just before serving. Garnish with lime slices. *Makes 8 servings*

Nutrients per serving:

Calories	184	Cholesterol	23 mg
Fat	4 g	Sodium	1209 mg

Favorite recipe from **USA Rice Council**

Hearty Chicken and Rice Soup

Entrées

Left: Chicken Picante
Right: Southwestern Stir-Fry (page 40)

CHICKEN PICANTE

- **½ cup medium-hot chunky taco sauce**
- **¼ cup Dijon-style mustard**
- **2 tablespoons fresh lime juice**
- **3 whole chicken breasts, split, skinned and boned**
- **2 tablespoons butter or margarine**
- **Chopped cilantro for garnish**
- **Plain nonfat yogurt**

Combine taco sauce, mustard and lime juice in large bowl. Add chicken, turning to coat. Cover; marinate in refrigerator at least 30 minutes.

Melt butter in large skillet over medium heat until foamy. Remove chicken from marinade; reserve marinade. Add chicken to skillet; cook about 10 minutes or until brown on both sides. Add marinade; cook about 5 minutes or until chicken is tender and marinade glazes chicken. Remove chicken to serving platter. Boil marinade over high heat 1 minute; pour over chicken. Garnish with cilantro. Serve with yogurt.

Makes 6 servings

Nutrients per serving:

Calories	194	Cholesterol	73 mg
Fat	8 g	Sodium	329 mg

Favorite recipe from **National Broiler Council**

Oriental Seafood Stir-Fry

ORIENTAL SEAFOOD STIR–FRY

½ cup water
3 tablespoons REALEMON® Lemon Juice from Concentrate
3 tablespoons soy sauce
1 tablespoon brown sugar
1 tablespoon cornstarch
2 ounces fresh pea pods
¾ cup sliced fresh mushrooms
¾ cup diced red bell pepper
1 medium onion, cut into wedges
1 tablespoon vegetable oil
½ pound imitation crab blend, flaked
Shredded napa (Chinese cabbage), angel hair pasta or rice noodles

In small bowl, combine water, ReaLemon® brand, soy sauce, sugar and cornstarch. In large skillet or wok, over medium-high heat, cook and stir vegetables in oil until tender-crisp; remove. Add soy mixture; over medium heat, cook and stir until slightly thickened. Add vegetables and crab blend; heat through. Serve with napa, pasta or rice noodles. Refrigerate leftovers.

Makes 4 servings

Nutrients per serving:

Calories	151	Cholesterol	11 mg
Fat	4 g	Sodium	1266 mg

SOUTHWESTERN STIR–FRY

1 pound pork tenderloin
2 tablespoons dry sherry
2 tablespoons cornstarch
1 teaspoon ground cumin
1 clove garlic, finely chopped
½ teaspoon seasoned salt
1 tablespoon vegetable oil
1 medium onion, thinly sliced
1 medium green bell pepper, cut into strips
12 cherry tomatoes, halved
Warm flour tortillas and green chili salsa for serving

Cut pork tenderloin lengthwise into quarters. Cut each quarter into ¼-inch-thick slices. Combine sherry, cornstarch, cumin, garlic and seasoned salt in medium bowl. Add pork slices; stir to coat.

Heat oil in large, heavy skillet over medium-high heat. Add pork mixture; stir-fry 3 to 4 minutes. Stir in onion, pepper and tomatoes. Reduce heat to low; cover and simmer 3 to 4 minutes. Serve hot with tortillas and salsa.

Makes 5 servings

Nutrients per serving:

Calories	180	Cholesterol	41 mg
Fat	9 g	Sodium	255 mg

Favorite recipe from **National Pork Producers**

FIESTA TURKEY PIE

- **1 package (about 1 pound) LOUIS RICH® Fresh Ground Turkey**
- **1 cup salsa**
- **1 can (8 ounces) refrigerated crescent dinner rolls**
- **¼ cup shredded sharp Cheddar cheese**

Preheat oven to 450°F. Cook turkey in nonstick skillet over medium heat about 10 minutes or until turkey is no longer pink, stirring to break turkey into small pieces. Stir in salsa.

Press crescent roll dough onto bottom, up side and on rim of 9-inch pie plate to form crust. Spread turkey mixture evenly over crust; sprinkle with cheese. Bake 18 to 20 minutes or until crust is browned.

Makes 6 to 8 servings

Nutrients per serving:

Calories	196	Cholesterol	35 mg
Fat	10 g	Sodium	413 mg

BLACK PEPPER PATTIES

- **1 package (about 1 pound) LOUIS RICH® Fresh Ground Turkey**
- **1 teaspoon instant chicken bouillon**
- **¼ teaspoon dried thyme leaves**
- **1 teaspoon coarse ground black pepper**

Sauce

- **1 large tomato, chopped**
- **½ cup plain nonfat yogurt**
- **1 tablespoon chopped fresh parsley**

Mix turkey, bouillon and thyme in bowl. Shape into four 4-inch patties. Sprinkle black pepper on patties (about ⅛ teaspoon per side), lightly pressing black pepper into turkey. Cook turkey in nonstick skillet over medium heat about 12 minutes or until no longer pink, turning occasionally.

Meanwhile, mix sauce ingredients in small bowl. Serve cold sauce over turkey patties. *Makes 4 servings*

Nutrients per serving (1 patty):

Calories	190	Cholesterol	75 mg
Fat	8 g	Sodium	315 mg

Top: Fiesta Turkey Pie
Bottom: Black Pepper Patties

DAD'S FAVORITE TURKEY KABOBS

3 ears corn, cut into 1-inch pieces
2 medium zucchini, cut into ¾-inch pieces
2 red bell peppers, cut into 1-inch cubes
2 Turkey Tenderloins (about 1 pound), cut into 1-inch cubes
⅓ cup reduced-calorie Italian salad dressing
Additional reduced calorie Italian salad dressing

1. In medium saucepan over high heat, blanch corn in boiling water about 1 to 2 minutes. Remove corn from saucepan and plunge into cold water.
2. In large glass bowl, place corn, zucchini, peppers, turkey and ⅓ cup dressing; cover and refrigerate 1 to 2 hours.
3. Drain turkey and vegetables, discarding marinade. Alternately thread turkey cubes and vegetables on skewers, leaving ½-inch space between turkey and vegetables.
4. On outdoor charcoal grill, cook kabobs 18 to 20 minutes, brushing with additional dressing. Turn skewers after first 10 minutes.

Makes 4 servings, 8 kabobs

Nutrients per serving (2 kabobs):

Calories	218	Cholesterol	70 mg
Fat	4 g	Sodium	381 mg

Favorite recipe from **National Turkey Federation**

Dad's Favorite Turkey Kabobs

FAST BEEF ROAST WITH MUSHROOM SAUCE

- 1 boneless beef rib eye roast (about 2 pounds)
- 2 tablespoons vegetable oil
- 4 cups water
- 1 can (10¾ ounces) condensed beef broth
- 1 cup dry red wine
- 2 cloves garlic, minced
- 1 teaspoon dried marjoram leaves
- 4 black peppercorns
- 3 whole cloves
- Mushroom Sauce (recipe follows)

Tie roast with heavy string at 2-inch intervals. Heat oil in Dutch oven over medium-high heat. Cook roast until evenly browned. Pour off drippings. Add water, broth, wine, garlic, marjoram, peppercorns and cloves; bring to a boil. Reduce heat to medium-low. Cover; simmer 15 minutes per pound. Check temperature with instant-read thermometer; temperature should be 130°F for rare. *Do not overcook.* Remove roast to serving platter; reserve cooking liquid. Cover roast tightly with plastic wrap or foil; allow to stand 10 minutes before carving (temperature will continue to rise about 10°F to 140°F for rare). Prepare Mushroom Sauce. Remove strings from roast. Carve into thin slices and top with Mushroom Sauce. Serve with assorted vegetables, if desired.

Makes 6 to 8 servings

Note: A boneless beef rib eye roast will yield three to four 3-ounce cooked servings per pound.

Fast Beef Roast with Mushroom Sauce

MUSHROOM SAUCE

- 1 tablespoon butter
- 1 cup sliced fresh mushrooms
- 1 cup beef cooking liquid, strained
- 1½ teaspoons cornstarch
- ¼ teaspoon salt
- 2 dashes pepper
- 1 tablespoon thinly sliced green onion tops

Melt butter in medium saucepan over medium-high heat. Add mushrooms; cook and stir 5 minutes. Remove and reserve. Add cooking liquid, cornstarch, salt and pepper to pan. Bring to a boil; cook and stir until thickened, 1 to 2 minutes. Remove from heat. Stir in reserved mushrooms and green onion.

Nutrients per serving (includes 3 tablespoons sauce):

Calories	188	Cholesterol	59 mg
Fat	8 g	Sodium	327 mg

Favorite recipe from **National Livestock and Meat Board**

Wisconsin Tuna Cakes with Lemon-Dill Sauce

WISCONSIN TUNA CAKES WITH LEMON–DILL SAUCE

1 can (12½ ounces) STARKIST® Tuna, drained and finely flaked
¾ cup seasoned bread crumbs
¼ cup minced green onions
2 tablespoons chopped drained pimento
1 egg
½ cup low-fat milk
½ teaspoon grated lemon peel
2 tablespoons margarine or butter

Lemon-Dill Sauce
¼ cup chicken broth
1 tablespoon lemon juice
¼ teaspoon dried dill weed
Hot steamed shredded zucchini and carrots
Lemon slices

In large bowl, toss together tuna, bread crumbs, onions and pimento. In small bowl, beat together egg and milk; stir in lemon peel. Stir into tuna mixture; toss until moistened. With lightly floured hands, shape mixture into eight 4-inch patties.

In large nonstick skillet, melt margarine. Fry patties, a few at a time, until golden brown on both sides, about 3 minutes per side. Place on ovenproof platter in 300°F oven until ready to serve.

For Lemon-Dill Sauce, in small saucepan, heat broth, lemon juice and dill. Serve tuna cakes with zucchini and carrots; spoon sauce over cakes. Garnish with lemon slices.

Makes 4 servings

Nutrients per serving (2 patties plus 1 tablespoon sauce):

Calories	278	Cholesterol	85 mg
Fat	10 g	Sodium	576 mg

SUNDAY SUPER STUFFED SHELLS

3 cloves fresh garlic
2 tablespoons olive oil
¾ pound ground veal
¾ pound ground pork
1 package (10 ounces) frozen chopped spinach, cooked, drained and squeezed dry
1 cup parsley, finely chopped
1 cup bread crumbs
2 eggs, beaten
3 cloves fresh garlic, minced
3 tablespoons grated Parmesan cheese
Salt to taste
1 package (12 ounces) uncooked jumbo pasta shells, cooked, rinsed and drained
3 cups spaghetti sauce
Sautéed zucchini slices (optional)

Cook and stir 3 whole garlic cloves in hot oil in large skillet over medium heat until garlic is browned. Discard garlic. Add veal and pork. Cook until lightly browned, stirring to separate meat; drain fat. Set aside.

Combine spinach, parsley, bread crumbs, eggs, minced garlic and cheese in large bowl; blend well. Season to taste with salt. Add cooled meat mixture; blend well. Fill shells with stuffing.

Spread about 1 cup spaghetti sauce over bottom of greased 12×8-inch pan. Arrange shells in pan. Pour remaining sauce over shells. Cover with foil. Bake in preheated 375°F oven 35 to 45 minutes or until bubbly. Serve with zucchini. Garnish as desired. *Makes 9 to 12 servings*

Nutrients per serving:

Calories	290	Cholesterol	81 mg
Fat	10 g	Sodium	428 mg

Favorite recipe from **Fresh Garlic Association**

Sunday Super Stuffed Shells

PORK TENDERLOIN DIANE

1 pound pork tenderloin, cut crosswise into 8 pieces
2 teaspoons lemon pepper
2 tablespoons butter
2 tablespoons lemon juice
1 tablespoon Worcestershire sauce
1 teaspoon Dijon-style mustard
1 tablespoon finely chopped chives or parsley
Whole chives for garnish

Press each tenderloin piece into 1-inch-thick medallion; sprinkle surfaces with lemon pepper. Melt butter in large heavy skillet over medium heat. Add medallions; cook 3 to 4 minutes on each side. Remove pork to serving platter; keep warm. Stir lemon juice, Worcestershire sauce and mustard into pan juices in skillet. Cook, stirring, until heated through. Pour sauce over medallions; sprinkle with chopped chives. Garnish with whole chives. Serve with vegetables.

Makes 5 servings

Nutrients per serving:

Calories	198	Cholesterol	84 mg
Fat	9 g	Sodium	157 mg

Favorite recipe from **National Pork Producers**

Pork Tenderloin Diane

BROILED ORIENTAL FISH

¼ cup CRISCO® PURITAN® Oil
¼ cup reduced-sodium soy sauce
¼ cup dry white wine
1½ teaspoons sesame seeds
1 teaspoon sugar
½ teaspoon ground ginger
1 pound Dover sole fillets
12 green onions
½ teaspoon pepper (optional)

1. Heat broiler. Combine Crisco® Puritan® Oil, soy sauce, wine, sesame seeds, sugar and ginger in shallow baking dish. Stir until blended.

2. Place fillets in marinade. Turn to coat. Marinate 20 minutes. Turn occasionally.

3. Wash green onions. Trim tops so onions are 5 to 6 inches in length. Make 3-inch slices in onion tops to give onions feathered look.

4. Place onions in marinade for last 10 minutes of marinating time.

5. Remove fish and onions from marinade. Place on broiler pan. Sprinkle with pepper, if desired. Place pan in oven 4 to 5 inches from heat.

6. Broil 3 minutes. Turn fish and onions carefully using pancake turner and broil 3 minutes more or until fish flakes easily when tested with fork. *Makes 4 servings*

To Microwave: Follow steps 2, 3 and 4. Remove fish and onions from marinade. Place in 12×8-inch microwave-safe dish. Sprinkle with pepper, if desired. Cover with plastic wrap. Microwave on HIGH 2 minutes. Rotate dish. Microwave on HIGH 1½ minutes or until fish flakes easily when tested with fork. Let stand, covered, 1 minute.

Nutrients per serving:

Calories	190	Cholesterol	75 mg
Fat	9 g	Sodium	180 mg

Chicken with Pineapple Salsa

CHICKEN WITH PINEAPPLE SALSA

1 can (20 ounces) DOLE® Crushed Pineapple in Juice
4 boneless skinless chicken breast halves
1 large clove garlic, pressed
1 teaspoon ground cumin
Salt and black pepper to taste
1 tablespoon vegetable oil
½ cup minced DOLE® Red Bell Pepper
¼ cup minced DOLE® Green Bell Pepper
1 tablespoon minced DOLE® Green Onion
2 teaspoons minced cilantro
2 teaspoons minced fresh or canned jalapeño chilies
1 teaspoon lime zest

- Drain pineapple; reserve juice.
- Rub chicken with garlic; sprinkle with cumin, salt and black pepper. In 12-inch skillet, sauté chicken in hot oil over medium-high heat until browned; turn once. Add ½ cup pineapple juice to chicken. Reduce heat. Cover; simmer 7 to 10 minutes.
- For salsa, combine pineapple, remaining reserved juice and remaining ingredients in bowl.
- Cut each breast into slices. Serve chicken with salsa. Garnish as desired. *Makes 4 servings*

Prep time: 5 minutes
Cook time: 15 minutes

Nutrients per serving:

Calories	262	Cholesterol	68 mg
Fat	5 g	Sodium	81 mg

Scallop Kabobs

SCALLOP KABOBS

¼ cup REALEMON® Lemon Juice from Concentrate
2 tablespoons vegetable oil
1 teaspoon dried oregano leaves
½ teaspoon dried basil leaves
1 clove garlic, finely chopped
⅛ teaspoon salt
1 pound sea scallops
8 ounces fresh mushrooms
2 small zucchini, cut into chunks
2 small onions, cut into wedges
½ red, yellow or green bell pepper, cut into bite-size pieces
Additional REALEMON® Brand

In shallow dish, combine ReaLemon® brand, oil and seasonings; add scallops. Cover; marinate in refrigerator 2 hours, stirring occasionally. Remove scallops from marinade; discard marinade. Thread scallops onto 8 skewers alternately with vegetables. Grill or broil as desired, basting frequently with additional ReaLemon® brand. Refrigerate leftovers.

Makes 8 kabobs

Nutrients per serving (2 kabobs):

Calories	213	Cholesterol	37 mg
Fat	8 g	Sodium	255 mg

CHICKEN BREASTS FLORENTINE

6 boneless skinless chicken breast halves (about 1½ pounds)
1 package (10 ounces) frozen chopped spinach, thawed, squeezed dry
1 jar (2½ ounces) sliced mushrooms, drained
½ cup chopped onion
½ cup shredded low-fat mozzarella cheese
½ cup low-fat ricotta cheese
⅛ teaspoon pepper
1 jar (12 ounces) HEINZ® HomeStyle Chicken Gravy
½ teaspoon dried thyme leaves, crushed

Place chicken breasts in lightly greased 13×9-inch baking pan. Combine spinach, mushrooms, onion, cheeses and pepper in medium bowl. Spoon spinach mixture on top of chicken breasts. Combine gravy and thyme; spoon over spinach and chicken. Cover; bake in 375°F oven 40 to 45 minutes.

Makes 6 servings

To Microwave: Place chicken breasts in 13×9-inch microwave-safe baking dish. Combine spinach, mushrooms, onion, cheeses and pepper in medium bowl. Spoon spinach mixture on top of chicken breasts. Combine gravy and thyme; spoon over spinach and chicken. Cover dish with waxed paper. Microwave at HIGH 18 to 20 minutes or until chicken is no longer pink, rearranging halfway through cooking.

Nutrients per serving:

Calories	227	Cholesterol	77 mg
Fat	7 g	Sodium	573 mg

RHUBARB PORK LOIN

1 boneless pork loin roast (3 pounds), rolled
1 clove garlic, cut into 8 to 10 slivers
1 teaspoon dried rosemary, crushed
4 stalks rhubarb, sliced (about 2 cups)
¼ cup plus 2 tablespoons honey
¼ cup cider vinegar
6 whole cloves
½ teaspoon salt
½ teaspoon dry mustard
2 to 3 drops red food coloring (optional)

Preheat oven to 350°F. Place pork roast in roasting pan. Cut 8 to 10 slits in surface of pork and insert garlic slivers. Rub entire surface of roast with rosemary. Insert meat thermometer so bulb is centered in thickest part, not resting in fat. Roast 1 hour.

Meanwhile, combine remaining ingredients in small, heavy saucepan. Bring to a boil over high heat. Reduce heat to low. Simmer 10 minutes. Remove and discard whole cloves. Pour rhubarb sauce over pork; continue to roast, basting often, for about 45 minutes or until roast reaches an internal temperature of 155°F. Let stand 10 minutes to allow internal temperature to rise to 160°F. Carve into thin slices. Heat rhubarb sauce remaining in roasting pan; serve with pork. Serve with vegetable. Garnish as desired. *Makes 10 servings*

Nutrients per serving:

Calories	208	Cholesterol	61 mg
Fat	9 g	Sodium	162 mg

Favorite recipe from **National Pork Producers**

Rhubarb Pork Loin

PAELLA

- **1 tablespoon olive oil**
- **½ pound chicken breast cubes**
- **1 cup uncooked long-grain white rice***
- **1 medium onion, chopped**
- **1 clove garlic, minced**
- **1½ cups chicken broth***
- **1 can (8 ounces) stewed tomatoes, chopped, reserving liquid**
- **½ teaspoon paprika**
- **⅛ to ¼ teaspoon ground red pepper**
- **⅛ teaspoon ground saffron**
- **½ pound medium shrimp, peeled and deveined**
- **1 small red pepper, cut into strips**
- **1 small green pepper, cut into strips**
- **½ cup frozen green peas**

Heat oil in Dutch oven over medium-high heat until hot. Add chicken and stir until browned. Add rice, onion, and garlic. Cook, stirring, until onion is tender and rice is lightly browned. Add broth, tomatoes, tomato liquid, paprika, ground red pepper, and saffron. Bring to a boil over high heat; stir. Reduce heat to low; cover and simmer 10 minutes. Add shrimp, pepper strips, and peas. Cover and simmer 10 minutes or until rice is tender and liquid is absorbed.

Makes 6 servings

*If using medium grain rice, use 1¼ cups broth; if using parboiled rice, use 1¾ cups broth.

Nutrients per serving:

Calories	253	Cholesterol	82 mg
Fat	4 g	Sodium	392 mg

Favorite recipe from **USA Rice Council**

LINGUINE PRIMAVERA

- **2 tablespoons olive or vegetable oil**
- **2 tablespoons lemon juice**
- **1 medium red pepper, cut into strips**
- **1 large onion, chopped**
- **1 package (8 ounces) fresh mushrooms, sliced**
- **½ pound lean fully cooked ham, cut into julienne strips**
- **1 package (10 ounces) frozen peas, thawed**
- **1 package (6 ounces) frozen snow peas, thawed**
- **1 can (5 ounces) evaporated skimmed milk**
- **½ cup shredded Provolone cheese, divided**
- **½ of (1-pound) package CREAMETTE® Linguine**
- **Freshly ground black pepper**

In large skillet, heat olive oil and lemon juice. Add red pepper, onion and mushrooms; cook until tender-crisp. Add ham, peas, milk and ¼ cup cheese; heat through, stirring frequently. Keep warm. Prepare Creamette® Linguine according to package directions; drain. Combine hot cooked linguine and vegetable mixture; toss to coat. Top with remaining ¼ cup cheese. Serve immediately with freshly ground black pepper. Refrigerate leftovers.

Makes 8 servings

Nutrients per serving:

Calories	273	Cholesterol	22 mg
Fat	8 g	Sodium	493 mg

Turkey and Rice Quiche

TURKEY AND RICE QUICHE

3 cups cooked rice, cooled to room temperature
1½ cups chopped cooked turkey
1 medium tomato, seeded and finely diced
¼ cup sliced green onions
¼ cup finely diced green pepper
1 tablespoon chopped fresh basil *or* 1 teaspoon dried basil
½ teaspoon seasoned salt
⅛ to ¼ teaspoon ground red pepper
½ cup skim milk
3 eggs, beaten
Nonstick cooking spray
½ cup (2 ounces) shredded Cheddar cheese
½ cup (2 ounces) shredded mozzarella cheese

Combine rice, turkey, tomato, onions, green pepper, basil, salt, ground red pepper, milk, and eggs in 13×9-inch pan coated with nonstick cooking spray. Top with cheeses. Bake at 375°F for 20 minutes or until knife inserted near center comes out clean. To serve, cut quiche into 8 squares; cut each square diagonally into 2 triangles. Garnish as desired.

Makes 8 servings, 16 triangles

Nutrients per serving (2 triangles):

Calories	231	Cholesterol	111 mg
Fat	7 g	Sodium	527 mg

Favorite recipe from **USA Rice Council**

Vegetables and Side Dishes

Left: Pasta Delight (page 57)
Right: Tomatoes with Basil Cream

TOMATOES WITH BASIL CREAM

1 clove garlic
1 container (8 ounces) Light PHILADELPHIA BRAND® Pasteurized Process Cream Cheese Product
2 tablespoons white wine vinegar
2 tablespoons chopped fresh basil
2 tablespoons chopped fresh parsley, divided
½ teaspoon salt
¼ teaspoon pepper
2 red tomatoes, thinly sliced
2 yellow tomatoes, thinly sliced

- Place garlic in blender or food processor container; cover. Process until finely chopped.
- Add cream cheese product, vinegar, basil, 1 tablespoon parsley, salt and pepper; blend until smooth.
- Arrange tomatoes on serving platter. Spoon cream cheese mixture over tomatoes. Sprinkle with remaining 1 tablespoon parsley. Garnish with fresh basil leaves, if desired.

Makes 10 servings

Prep time: 15 minutes

Nutrients per serving:

Calories	60	Cholesterol	15 mg
Fat	trace	Sodium	240 mg

GREEN BEANS WITH PINE NUTS

1 pound green beans, ends removed
2 tablespoons butter or margarine
2 tablespoons pine nuts
Salt
Pepper

Cook beans in 1 inch water in covered 3-quart saucepan 4 to 8 minutes or until crisp-tender; drain. Melt butter in large skillet over medium heat. Add pine nuts; cook, stirring frequently, until golden. Add beans; stir gently to coat beans with butter. Season with salt and pepper to taste.

Makes 4 servings

Nutrients per serving:

Calories	127	Cholesterol	0 mg
Fat	10 g	Sodium	1 mg

Green Beans with Pine Nuts

FRESH CORN WITH ADOBE BUTTER

Chili powder and lime juice make sweet corn taste even sweeter.

½ teaspoon chili powder
1 teaspoon lime juice
¼ cup butter or margarine, softened
Salt
4 ears yellow or white corn, husks and silk removed

Moisten chili powder with lime juice in small bowl. Add butter; stir until well blended. Season with salt to taste. Place in small crock or bowl. Place corn in 5-quart pan; cover with cold water. Cover pan and bring to a boil. Boil 1 minute. Turn off heat; let stand 2 minutes or until corn is tender. Drain. Serve with Adobe Butter.

Makes 4 servings

Nutrients per serving (1 ear corn with ½ tablespoon Adobe Butter):

Calories	134	Cholesterol	0 mg
Fat	6 g	Sodium	74 mg

"LITE" APRICOT STUFFING

1 cup sliced celery
¾ cup chopped onion
1½ cups turkey broth or reduced-sodium chicken broth
16 slices reduced-calorie bread, cubed and dried
2 tablespoons parsley flakes
1½ teaspoons poultry seasoning
½ teaspoon salt
2 egg whites
¼ cup dried apricots, chopped

Corn Olé

In small saucepan, over medium-high heat, combine celery, onion and turkey broth; bring to a boil. Reduce heat to low; cover and simmer 5 minutes or until vegetables are tender.

In large bowl, combine celery mixture, bread cubes, parsley, poultry seasoning, salt, egg whites and apricots. Spoon into lightly greased 2-quart casserole; cover. Bake at 350°F for 30 minutes or until heated through. *Makes 8 servings*

Nutrients per serving:

Calories	164	Cholesterol	trace
Fat	2 g	Sodium	566 mg

Favorite recipe from **National Turkey Federation**

CORN OLÉ

2 tablespoons butter or margarine
3 cups chopped fresh tomatoes
2 cups fresh corn, cut off the cob (about 4 ears)
2 cups (about ¾ pound) summer squash slices, halved
⅓ cup chopped onion
¼ teaspoon pepper

Melt butter in large skillet. Add remaining ingredients; cover. Cook 10 to 15 minutes or until squash is tender, stirring occasionally.

Makes 6 servings

Nutrients per serving:

Calories	111	Cholesterol	0 mg
Fat	5 g	Sodium	59 mg

ITALIAN CAPELLINI AND FRESH TOMATO

½ of a (1-pound) package CREAMETTE® Capellini, uncooked
2 cups peeled, seeded, finely chopped fresh tomatoes (about 3 medium)
2 tablespoons olive oil
1 teaspoon basil leaves
½ teaspoon salt
½ teaspoon coarse ground pepper

Prepare Creamette® Capellini according to package directions; drain. Quickly toss hot cooked capellini with remaining ingredients. Serve immediately. Refrigerate leftovers. *Makes 6 servings*

Nutrients per serving:

Calories	196	Cholesterol	0 mg
Fat	5 g	Sodium	170 mg

CINNAMON–APPLE SWEET POTATOES

4 medium sweet potatoes
1½ cups finely chopped apple
½ cup orange juice
¼ cup sugar
1½ teaspoons cornstarch
½ teaspoon ground cinnamon
½ teaspoon grated orange peel

To Microwave: Wash sweet potatoes and prick them with fork. Place on paper towels. Microwave on HIGH 10 to 13 minutes or until tender, turning halfway through cooking. Set aside. In microwave-safe bowl, combine remaining ingredients. Cover; cook on HIGH 3 minutes. Stir mixture; cook, uncovered, on HIGH 1½ to 2½ minutes more or until the sauce is thickened. Slit sweet potatoes and spoon sauce over each one. *Makes 4 servings*

Tip: Sauce can be made up ahead and reheated at serving time.

Nutrients per serving:

Calories	216	Cholesterol	0 mg
Fat	trace	Sodium	12 mg

Favorite recipe from **The Sugar Association, Inc.**

Cinnamon-Apple Sweet Potatoes

GLAZED STIR-FRY HOLIDAY VEGETABLES

2 tablespoons sugar
½ teaspoon grated lemon peel
3 tablespoons fresh lemon juice (1 lemon)
1 tablespoon low-sodium soy sauce
2 teaspoons cornstarch
½ cup water
4 teaspoons vegetable oil
3 cups fresh broccoli florets
1 medium red bell pepper, cut into 1-inch pieces
1 cup peeled, julienne-cut jicama
Lemon zest (slivers of lemon peel)

In small bowl combine sugar, lemon peel, lemon juice, soy sauce and cornstarch. Stir in water; set aside.

Heat oil in large nonstick skillet. Add broccoli and pepper and stir-fry over high heat 2 minutes. Add jicama and cook 1 to 2 more minutes or until vegetables are crisp-tender, adding additional oil, if necessary. Pour lemon mixture over vegetables and continue cooking just until glaze thickens. Toss vegetables to coat thoroughly with glaze. Garnish with lemon zest.

Makes 6 servings, 3 cups

Nutrients per serving (½ cup):

Calories	95	Cholesterol	0 mg
Fat	3 g	Sodium	72 mg

Favorite recipe from **The Sugar Association, Inc.**

Glazed Stir-Fry Holiday Vegetables

PASTA DELIGHT

1 medium zucchini, sliced
1 tablespoon olive oil
2 tablespoons chopped shallots
2 cloves garlic, chopped
1 medium tomato, diced
2 tablespoons chopped fresh basil *or* ½ teaspoon dried basil, crushed
2 tablespoons grated Parmesan cheese
12 ounces uncooked penne pasta, hot cooked and drained

Cook and stir zucchini in hot oil in large skillet over medium-high heat. Reduce heat to medium. Add shallots and garlic; cook 1 minute. Add tomato; cook and stir 45 seconds. Add basil and cheese. Pour vegetable mixture over penne in large bowl; toss gently to mix. *Makes 4 to 6 servings*

Nutrients per serving:

Calories	237	Cholesterol	51 mg
Fat	5 g	Sodium	51 mg

Favorite recipe from **National Pasta Association**

VEGETABLE SOUFFLÉ IN PEPPER CUPS

1 cup chopped broccoli
½ cup shredded carrot
¼ cup chopped onion
1 teaspoon dried basil leaves
½ teaspoon ground black pepper
2 teaspoons FLEISCHMANN'S® Margarine
2 tablespoons all-purpose flour
1 cup skim milk
1 container (8 ounces) EGG BEATERS® 99% Real Egg Product
3 large red, green or yellow peppers, halved lengthwise

In nonstick skillet, over medium-high heat, cook broccoli, carrot, onion, basil and black pepper in margarine until tender. Stir in flour until smooth. Gradually add milk, stirring constantly until thickened. Remove from heat; set aside.

In medium bowl, with electric mixer at high speed, beat Egg Beaters® until foamy, about 3 minutes. Gently fold into broccoli mixture; spoon into pepper halves. Place in 13×9-inch baking pan. Bake at 375°F for 30 to 35 minutes or until knife inserted in center comes out clean. Garnish and serve immediately.

Makes 6 servings

Nutrients per serving:

Calories	75	Cholesterol	1 mg
Fat	2 g	Sodium	91 mg

STUFFED TOMATOES

6 to 8 medium tomatoes
2 tablespoons CRISCO® PURITAN® Oil
⅓ cup chopped celery
2 tablespoons chopped onion
2 cups cooked brown rice
¼ cup grated Parmesan cheese
1 tablespoon snipped fresh parsley
1 teaspoon dried basil leaves
⅛ teaspoon pepper
⅛ teaspoon garlic powder

1. Cut thin slice from top of each tomato. Set aside. Scoop out centers of tomatoes; chop pulp and set aside. Place shells, upside-down, on paper towels to drain.

2. Preheat oven to 350°F. Heat Crisco® Puritan® Oil in medium saucepan. Add celery and onion. Sauté over moderate heat until celery is tender. Remove from heat. Add reserved tomato pulp, rice, Parmesan cheese, parsley, basil, pepper and garlic powder. Mix well. Fill each tomato shell with one-fourth rice mixture. Replace tomato tops, if desired.

3. Lightly oil 9-inch pie plate or round baking dish with Crisco® Puritan® Oil. Place tomatoes in dish. Cover with aluminum foil.

4. Bake at 350°F for 30 to 45 minutes, or until tomatoes are tender. *Makes 6 to 8 servings*

Note: Use 1 lightly oiled custard cup for each tomato instead of pie plate or baking dish, if desired.

Nutrients per serving:

Calories	125	Cholesterol	2 mg
Fat	5 g	Sodium	65 mg

Spinach Feta Rice

SPINACH FETA RICE

- **1 cup uncooked long-grain white rice**
- **1 cup chicken broth**
- **1 cup water**
- **1 medium onion, chopped**
- **1 cup (about 4 ounces) sliced fresh mushrooms**
- **2 cloves garlic, minced**
- **Nonstick cooking spray**
- **1 tablespoon lemon juice**
- **½ teaspoon dried oregano leaves**
- **6 cups shredded fresh spinach leaves (about ¼ pound)**
- **4 ounces feta cheese, crumbled**
- **Freshly ground black pepper**
- **Chopped pimiento for garnish (optional)**

Combine rice, broth, and water in medium saucepan. Bring to a boil; stir once or twice. Reduce heat; cover and simmer 15 minutes or until rice is tender and liquid is absorbed. Cook onion, mushrooms, and garlic in large skillet coated with nonstick cooking spray until onion is tender. Add mushroom mixture, lemon juice, oregano, spinach, cheese, and black pepper to hot cooked rice; toss lightly until spinach is wilted. Garnish with pimiento. *Makes 6 servings*

To Microwave: Combine rice, broth, and water in deep 2- to 3-quart microproof baking dish. Cover and cook on HIGH 5 minutes. Reduce setting to MEDIUM (50% power) and cook 15 minutes or until rice is tender and liquid is absorbed. Combine onion, mushrooms, and garlic in 1-quart microproof baking dish coated with nonstick cooking spray. Cook on HIGH 2 to 3 minutes. Add mushroom mixture, lemon juice, oregano, spinach, cheese, and black pepper to hot cooked rice. Cook on HIGH 1 to 2 minutes or until spinach is wilted. Garnish with pimiento.

Nutrients per serving:

Calories	195	Cholesterol	17 mg
Fat	5 g	Sodium	387 mg

Favorite recipe from **USA Rice Council**

CREOLE STUFFED PEPPERS

6 large green peppers
Boiling water
½ cup chopped onion
1 tablespoon butter or margarine
2 cups chopped fresh tomatoes
2 cups fresh okra slices
2 cups fresh corn, cut off the cob (about 4 ears)
⅛ teaspoon black pepper

Preheat oven to 350°F. Cut off tops of green peppers; remove seeds. Add green peppers to boiling water in large saucepan; cover. Boil 5 minutes; drain. Cool. Sauté onion in butter. Add tomatoes, okra, corn and black pepper; cook until mixture is thoroughly heated and slightly thickened. Fill green peppers with corn mixture; place in greased shallow baking dish. Bake 30 minutes or until green peppers are tender.

Makes 6 servings

Nutrients per serving:

Calories	119	Cholesterol	0 mg
Fat	3 g	Sodium	39 mg

SUN VALLEY POTATO FRIES

2 large baking potatoes
¼ cup HELLMANN'S® or BEST FOODS® Light Reduced Calorie Mayonnaise

Preheat oven to 400°F. Cut potatoes into ¼-inch sticks. Spoon mayonnaise into large plastic food bag. Add potatoes; shake to coat well. Arrange in single layer in jelly-roll pan so potatoes do not touch. If desired, sprinkle with salt to taste. Bake 20 minutes or until golden brown and crisp, turning once with spatula.

Makes 6 servings

Nutrients per serving:

Calories	75	Cholesterol	3 mg
Fat	3 g	Sodium	3 mg

GRILLED VEGETABLE KABOBS

12 large fresh mushrooms
Boiling water
¼ cup Italian dressing
2 tablespoons lemon juice
1½ teaspoons Worcestershire sauce
2 medium zucchini, cut into 1-inch diagonal slices
4 cherry tomatoes

Place mushrooms in medium bowl; cover with boiling water. Let stand 1 minute; drain. Combine dressing, lemon juice and Worcestershire sauce in small bowl. Alternately thread mushrooms and zucchini on four skewers. Grill kabobs over medium coals about 10 minutes, turning and brushing frequently with dressing mixture. Remove from heat. Thread cherry tomatoes onto ends of skewers. Continue grilling 5 minutes, turning and brushing with remaining dressing mixture. Garnish as desired.

Makes 4 servings

Nutrients per serving:

Calories	44	Cholesterol	1 mg
Fat	2 g	Sodium	141 mg

Top left: Grilled Vegetable Kabobs
Bottom right: Creole Stuffed Peppers

RISOTTO WITH PEAS AND MUSHROOMS

½ cup chopped onion
2 teaspoons margarine
1 cup uncooked rice
⅓ cup dry white wine
1 cup chicken broth
4 cups water
1 cup frozen peas, thawed
1 jar (2½ ounces) sliced mushrooms, drained
¼ cup grated Parmesan cheese
¼ teaspoon ground white pepper
⅓ cup 2% low-fat milk

Cook onion in margarine in skillet over medium-high heat until soft. Add rice, stirring constantly 2 to 3 minutes. Add wine; stir until absorbed. Stir in broth. Cook, uncovered, stirring constantly, until broth is absorbed. Continue stirring and adding water, one cup at a time; allow each cup to be absorbed before adding another, until rice is tender and has a creamy consistency, 20 to 25 minutes. Stir in remaining ingredients. Stir until creamy, 1 to 2 minutes. Serve immediately.

Makes 6 servings

Tip: Medium grain rice will yield the best consistency for risottos, but long grain rice can be used.

Nutrients per serving:

Calories	205	Cholesterol	4 mg
Fat	6 g	Sodium	316 mg

Favorite recipe from **USA Rice Council**

Risotto with Peas and Mushrooms

SHRIMP STUFFING

1 pound raw shrimp, cleaned, quartered
2 tablespoons margarine
1 package (6 ounces) KELLOGG'S® CROUTETTES® Stuffing Mix
½ cup chopped celery
½ cup sliced green onions
¼ cup chopped green pepper
1 can (10¾ ounces) condensed cream of mushroom soup
¾ cup water
1 teaspoon dry mustard
1 teaspoon lemon juice
½ teaspoon Cajun seasoning
¼ teaspoon salt (optional)
½ cup (2 ounces) shredded part-skim mozzarella cheese

1. In 12-inch skillet, cook shrimp in margarine over medium heat just until shrimp start to change color.
2. Stir in remaining ingredients *except* cheese, tossing gently to moisten. Reduce heat to low. Cover and cook 5 minutes. Remove from heat and stir in cheese.

Makes 8 servings

To Microwave: In 4-quart microwave-safe mixing bowl, melt margarine at HIGH 1 minute. Combine remaining ingredients *except* cheese. Cover with plastic wrap, leaving a corner open as a vent. Microwave at HIGH 9 minutes or until stuffing is hot and shrimp are cooked, stirring every 3 minutes. (When stirring stuffing, carefully remove plastic from bowl to allow steam to escape.) Stir in cheese.

Nutrients per serving:

Calories	220	Cholesterol	95 mg
Fat	7 g	Sodium	827 mg

DILLED NEW POTATOES AND PEAS

1 pound (6 to 8) small new potatoes, quartered
2 cups frozen peas
1 jar (12 ounces) HEINZ® HomeStyle Turkey Gravy
½ cup light dairy sour cream
1 teaspoon dried dill weed

Cook potatoes in 2-quart saucepan in lightly salted boiling water 10 to 15 minutes or until tender. Add peas; cook 1 minute. Drain well. Combine gravy, sour cream and dill; stir into vegetable mixture. Heat, stirring occasionally.

Makes 8 servings, about 4 cups

To Microwave: Place potatoes and 2 tablespoons water in 2-quart casserole. Cover with lid or vented plastic wrap. Microwave at HIGH 6 to 7 minutes or until potatoes are just tender, stirring once. Stir in peas. Cover and microwave at HIGH 1 minute. Combine gravy, sour cream and dill; stir in vegetable mixture. Cover and microwave at HIGH 7 to 8 minutes or until heated through, stirring once.

Nutrients per serving (about ½ cup):

Calories	126	Cholesterol	6 mg
Fat	1 g	Sodium	332 mg

Salads

Left: Sesame Pork Salad
Right: Lemon Ginger Sauce (page 66)

SESAME PORK SALAD

3 cups cooked rice
1½ cups slivered cooked pork*
¼ pound fresh snow peas, trimmed and julienned
1 medium cucumber, peeled, seeded, and julienned
1 medium red pepper, julienned
½ cup sliced green onions
2 tablespoons sesame seeds, toasted (optional)
¼ cup chicken broth
3 tablespoons rice or white wine vinegar
3 tablespoons soy sauce
1 tablespoon peanut oil
1 teaspoon sesame oil

Combine rice, pork, snow peas, cucumber, pepper, onions, and sesame seeds in large bowl. Combine broth, vinegar, soy sauce, and oils in small jar with lid. Pour over rice mixture; toss lightly. Serve at room temperature or slightly chilled.

Makes 6 servings

*Substitute 1½ cups slivered cooked chicken for pork, if desired.

Nutrients per serving:

Calories	269	Cholesterol	32 mg
Fat	8 g	Sodium	867 mg

Favorite recipe from **USA Rice Council**

Orange Salad with Cinnamon Dressing

ORANGE SALAD WITH CINNAMON DRESSING

8 oranges, peeled, sliced
4 cups torn assorted greens
Cinnamon Dressing (recipe follows)

- Arrange orange slices and greens on individual salad plates. Serve with Cinnamon Dressing. Garnish with orange peel, if desired.

Makes 8 servings

CINNAMON DRESSING

1 package (8 ounces) Light PHILADELPHIA BRAND® Neufchatel Cheese, softened
⅓ cup orange juice
1 tablespoon honey
1½ teaspoons grated orange peel
½ teaspoon ground cinnamon

- Place ingredients in blender or food processor container; cover. Blend until smooth.

Prep time: 20 minutes

Nutrients per serving:

Calories	160	Cholesterol	40 mg
Fat	7 g	Sodium	120 mg

LEMON GINGER SAUCE

½ cup MIRACLE WHIP® FREE® Nonfat Dressing
2 tablespoons lemon juice
1½ tablespoons packed brown sugar
1 teaspoon grated lemon peel
1 teaspoon ground ginger

- Mix together ingredients until well blended; refrigerate. Serve over fresh fruit.

Makes ½ cup

Prep time: 5 minutes plus refrigerating

Nutrients per serving (2 tablespoons):

Calories	70	Cholesterol	1 mg
Fat	trace	Sodium	422 mg

SOUTHWEST SALSA DRESSING

⅔ cup mild salsa*
2 tablespoons nonfat plain yogurt
4 teaspoons sugar
2 teaspoons chopped cilantro (optional)

In small bowl, stir together all ingredients. Or, for a less chunky dressing, blend together in food processor. Chill or serve immediately over green salad, chicken or turkey salad, taco salad or seafood salad.

Makes about 5 servings

*For a hotter and spicier dressing, use medium or hot salsa.

Nutrients per serving (2 tablespoons):

Calories	30	Cholesterol	trace
Fat	trace	Sodium	226 mg

Favorite recipe from **The Sugar Association, Inc.**

WHITE SANGRIA SPLASH

Wine adds a spirited touch to this festive salad. If you'd prefer, substitute fruit juice for the wine. This salad is also good with orange segments and chopped apple.

1½ cups dry white wine
2 packages (4-serving size) *or* 1 package (8-serving size) JELL-O® Brand Lemon Flavor Sugar Free Gelatin
2½ cups club soda
1 tablespoon lime juice
1 tablespoon orange liqueur (optional)
1 cup sliced strawberries
1 cup red grapes
1 cup green grapes

- Bring wine to boil in small saucepan. Pour boiling wine over gelatin in bowl; stir until completely dissolved. Stir in club soda, lime juice and liqueur, if desired. Place bowl in larger bowl of ice and water; let stand until slightly thickened, stirring occasionally, about 10 minutes.
- Gently stir in fruit. Pour into 6-cup mold which has been sprayed with nonstick cooking spray. Chill until firm, about 4 hours. Unmold.

Makes 12 servings, 6 cups

Nutrients per serving (½ cup):

Calories	50 mg	Cholesterol	0 mg
Fat	0 g	Sodium	55 mg

White Sangria Splash

SPARKLING BERRY SALAD

Club soda adds the "sparkle" to this fruit-packed salad. If you do not use the creme de cassis liqueur, add an extra ¼ cup of cranberry juice.

2 cups cranberry juice
2 packages (4-serving size) *or* 1 package (8-serving size) JELL-O® Brand Sugar Free Gelatin, any red flavor
1½ cups cold club soda
¼ cup creme de cassis liqueur (optional)
1 teaspoon lemon juice
1 cup sliced strawberries
1 cup raspberries
1 cup blueberries
Mint leaves (optional)

- Bring cranberry juice to boil in medium saucepan. Pour boiling cranberry juice over gelatin in bowl; stir until completely dissolved. Stir in club soda, liqueur and lemon juice. Chill until slightly thickened.
- Stir in 2 cups of the berries; reserve remaining 1 cup berries for garnish. Spoon into 6-cup mold which has been sprayed with nonstick cooking spray. Chill until firm, about 4 hours. Unmold. Garnish with reserved berries and mint leaves, if desired. *Makes 8 servings*

Nutrients per serving:

Calories	100	Cholesterol	0 mg
Fat	0 g	Sodium	70 mg

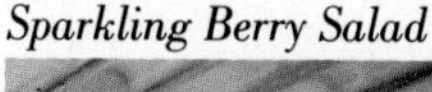

Sparkling Berry Salad

MARINATED VEGETABLE SPINACH SALAD

Mustard-Tarragon Marinade (recipe follows)
8 ounces fresh mushrooms, quartered
2 slices purple onion, separated into rings
16 cherry tomatoes, halved
4 cups fresh spinach leaves, washed and stems removed
3 slices (3 ounces) SARGENTO® Preferred Light Sliced Mozzarella Cheese, cut into julienne strips
Freshly ground black pepper

Prepare Mustard-Tarragon Marinade. Place mushrooms, onion and tomatoes in bowl. Toss with marinade and let stand 15 minutes. Arrange spinach on 4 individual plates. Divide marinated vegetables among plates and top each salad with one fourth of cheese. Serve with freshly ground black pepper, if desired. *Makes 4 servings*

MUSTARD-TARRAGON MARINADE

3 tablespoons red wine vinegar
1 tablespoon Dijon-style mustard
½ tablespoon dried tarragon
2 tablespoons olive oil

Combine first three ingredients in small bowl. Slowly whisk oil into mixture until slightly thickened.

Nutrients per serving:

Calories	186	Cholesterol	11 mg
Fat	10 g	Sodium	334 mg

SHELLS AND SHRIMP SALAD ALFRESCO

½ of (1-pound) package CREAMETTE® Medium Shells, uncooked
2 cups cooked medium shrimp, shelled, deveined
2 medium fresh tomatoes, peeled, seeded and chopped
2 cups torn fresh spinach
1 cup sliced fresh cauliflowerets
½ cup sliced radishes
¼ cup sliced green onions
2 tablespoons vegetable oil
2 tablespoons lemon juice
1 tablespoon Dijon-style mustard
¼ teaspoon thyme leaves, crushed
¼ teaspoon lemon pepper seasoning

Prepare Creamette® Medium Shells according to package directions; drain. In large bowl, combine shells, shrimp, tomatoes, spinach, cauliflowerets, radishes and green onions. In small bowl, blend oil, lemon juice, mustard, thyme and seasoning; add to salad and toss to coat. Cover; chill thoroughly. Toss gently before serving. Refrigerate leftovers. *Makes 10 servings*

Nutrients per serving:

Calories	176	Cholesterol	68 mg
Fat	4 g	Sodium	89 mg

POPPY SEED FRUIT SAUCE

½ cup MIRACLE WHIP® FREE® Nonfat Dressing
1 container (8 ounces) lemon-flavored low-fat yogurt
2 tablespoons skim milk
1 tablespoon packed brown sugar
1 tablespoon poppy seeds

- Mix together ingredients until well blended; refrigerate. Serve over fresh fruit. *Makes 1⅔ cups*

Prep time: 5 minutes

Nutrients per serving (3 tablespoons):

Calories	70	Cholesterol	trace
Fat	1 g	Sodium	263 mg

FETTUCCINI SLAW

½ of (1-pound) package CREAMETTE® Fettuccini, broken into thirds, uncooked
3 cups finely chopped cabbage
2 cups finely shredded carrots
2 cups thinly sliced celery
2 cups finely sliced cucumber
1 container (8 ounces) plain low-fat yogurt
½ cup reduced-calorie mayonnaise or salad dressing
2 tablespoons white vinegar
½ teaspoon dry mustard
¼ teaspoon white pepper
Paprika

Prepare Creamette® Fettuccini according to package directions; drain. In large bowl, combine fettuccini, cabbage, carrots, celery and cucumber. In small bowl, blend yogurt, mayonnaise, vinegar, mustard and pepper; toss with fettuccini mixture. Cover; chill thoroughly. Toss gently before serving. Garnish with paprika. Refrigerate leftovers.
Makes 12 servings

Nutrients per serving:

Calories	209	Cholesterol	4 mg
Fat	4 g	Sodium	105

TANGY TOMATO SALAD DRESSING

1 can (7¼ ounces) low-sodium tomato soup
¼ cup vegetable oil
Grated peel of ½ SUNKIST® Lemon
2 tablespoons fresh squeezed lemon juice
2 tablespoons chopped green onion
1 teaspoon prepared horseradish
Generous dash ground cinnamon (optional)

In jar with lid, combine all ingredients; chill. Shake well before serving. *Makes 1⅓ cups*

Nutrients per serving (1 tablespoon):

Calories	35	Cholesterol	0 mg
Fat	3 g	Sodium	2 mg

Poppy Seed Fruit Sauce

WILD RICE AND PEPPER SALAD

1 package (6 ounces) MINUTE® Long Grain & Wild Rice
½ cup MIRACLE WHIP® FREE® Nonfat Dressing
2 tablespoons olive oil
½ teaspoon black pepper
¼ teaspoon grated lemon peel
1 cup chopped red bell pepper
1 cup chopped yellow bell pepper
¼ cup ½-inch green onion pieces

- Prepare rice as directed on package. Cool.
- Mix dressing, oil, black pepper and peel until well blended.
- Add rice and remaining ingredients; mix lightly. Serve at room temperature or refrigerate.

Makes 6 servings

Prep time: 30 minutes

Nutrients per serving (½ cup):

Calories	140	Cholesterol	0 mg
Fat	5 g	Sodium	284 mg

Cucumber and Onion Salad

CUCUMBER AND ONION SALAD

½ cup MIRACLE WHIP® FREE® Nonfat Dressing
4 cucumbers, peeled, halved lengthwise, seeded, sliced
2 onions, sliced, halved
½ cup thin red bell pepper strips

- Mix together dressing, cucumbers and onions in large bowl. Top with peppers; refrigerate.

Makes 12 servings, 6 cups

Prep time: 10 minutes plus refrigerating

Nutrients per serving (½ cup):

Calories	30	Cholesterol	0 mg
Fat	trace	Sodium	143 mg

CHINESE CHICKEN SALAD

3 cups cooked rice, cooled
1 cup cooked chicken breast cubes
1 cup sliced celery
1 can (8 ounces) sliced water chestnuts, drained
1 cup fresh bean sprouts*
½ cup (about 2 ounces) sliced fresh mushrooms
¼ cup sliced green onions
¼ cup diced red pepper
3 tablespoons lemon juice
2 tablespoons reduced-sodium soy sauce
2 tablespoons sesame oil
2 teaspoons grated fresh ginger root
¼ to ½ teaspoon ground white pepper
Lettuce leaves

Lanai Pasta Salad

Combine rice, chicken, celery, water chestnuts, bean sprouts, mushrooms, onions, and red pepper in large bowl. Combine lemon juice, soy sauce, oil, ginger root, and white pepper in small jar with lid. Pour over rice mixture; toss lightly. Serve on lettuce leaves.

Makes 6 servings

*Substitute canned bean sprouts, rinsed and drained, for fresh bean sprouts, if desired.

Nutrients per serving:

Calories	248	Cholesterol	20 mg
Fat	6 g	Sodium	593 mg

Favorite recipe from **USA Rice Council**

LANAI PASTA SALAD

1 can (20 ounces) DOLE® Pineapple Chunks
3 cups cooked spiral pasta
2 cups sugar or snow peas
1 cup sliced DOLE® Carrots
1 cup sliced cucumbers
½ cup bottled reduced-calorie Italian salad dressing
¼ cup chopped cilantro or parsley

- Drain pineapple; reserve ¼ cup juice.
- Combine pineapple and reserved juice with remaining ingredients in large bowl; toss to coat.

Makes 6 to 8 servings

Nutrients per serving:

Calories	181	Cholesterol	0 mg
Fat	trace	Sodium	219 mg

Chef's Salad

CHUNKY CUCUMBER DILL DRESSING

1 cup peeled, chopped cucumber, divided
¾ cup plus 2 tablespoons nonfat plain yogurt
3 tablespoons fresh dill, chopped
2 teaspoons sugar
2 teaspoons lemon juice
⅛ teaspoon pepper

In blender or food processor, blend ½ cup cucumber with remaining ingredients. Stir in remaining ½ cup cucumber. Chill, then serve over green salad or chicken salad.

Makes about 6 servings

Nutrients per serving (2 tablespoons):

Calories	31	Cholesterol	1 mg
Fat	trace	Sodium	71 mg

Favorite recipe from **The Sugar Association, Inc.**

CHEF'S SALAD

1 package (4-serving size) JELL-O® Brand Lemon Flavor Sugar Free Gelatin
¼ teaspoon salt
¾ cup boiling water
½ cup cold water
Ice cubes
1 tablespoon vinegar
2 teaspoons reduced-calorie French dressing
¼ teaspoon Worcestershire sauce
⅛ teaspoon white pepper
¾ cup chopped tomato
½ cup finely shredded lettuce
½ cup slivered cooked turkey breast
½ cup slivered Swiss cheese
2 tablespoons chopped scallions
2 tablespoons chopped radishes

- Completely dissolve gelatin and salt in boiling water. Combine cold water and ice cubes to make 1¼ cups. Add to gelatin, stirring until slightly thickened. Remove any unmelted ice. Stir in vinegar, dressing, Worcestershire sauce and pepper. Chill until slightly thickened.
- Stir in vegetables, turkey and cheese. Spoon into 3 individual plastic containers or dishes. Chill until firm, about 2 hours.

Makes 3½ cups or 3 entrée servings

Nutrients per serving:

Calories	100	Cholesterol	30 mg
Fat	4 g	Sodium	330 mg

SALADE NIÇOISE

2 cans (6½ ounces each) tuna in water, drained, flaked
8 new potatoes, cooked, sliced
½ pound green beans, cooked
½ pound yellow wax beans, cooked
8 radishes, sliced
Niçoise or pitted ripe olives (optional)
Torn assorted greens
Herb Dressing (recipe follows)

- Arrange tuna, potatoes, beans, radishes, olives and greens on serving platter or individual plates. Serve with Herb Dressing.

Makes 8 servings

HERB DRESSING

¼ cup fresh basil leaves
1 tablespoon fresh parsley, stemmed
1 small shallot
1 container (8 ounces) Light PHILADELPHIA BRAND® Pasteurized Process Cream Cheese Product
⅓ cup skim milk
3 tablespoons white wine vinegar
½ teaspoon salt
½ teaspoon pepper

- Place basil, parsley and shallot in blender or food processor container; cover. Process until chopped. Add remaining ingredients; blend until smooth.

Prep time: 35 minutes

Nutrients per serving:

Calories	190	Cholesterol	94 mg
Fat	7 g	Sodium	500 mg

MOCK BLUE CHEESE DRESSING

¾ cup buttermilk
¼ cup low-fat cottage cheese
2 tablespoons blue cheese, crumbled
2 teaspoons sugar
1 teaspoon lemon juice
¼ teaspoon celery seed
⅛ teaspoon pepper
⅛ teaspoon salt
4 drops hot pepper sauce

In blender or food processor, blend all ingredients. Chill, then serve over green salad.

Makes 6 servings, ¾ cup

Nutrients per serving (2 tablespoons):

Calories	33	Cholesterol	3 mg
Fat	1 g	Sodium	148 mg

Favorite recipe from **The Sugar Association, Inc.**

Salade Niçoise

Desserts

Left: Mini-Almond Cheesecakes
Right: Orange Terrine with Strawberry Sauce (page 78)

MINI–ALMOND CHEESECAKES

¾ cup ground almonds
1 tablespoon PARKAY® Margarine, melted
1 envelope unflavored gelatin
¼ cup cold water
1 container (12 ounces) Light PHILADELPHIA BRAND® Pasteurized Process Cream Cheese Product, softened
¾ cup skim milk
½ cup sugar *or* 12 packets sugar substitute
¼ teaspoon almond extract
3 cups peeled peach slices

- Stir together almonds and margarine in small bowl. Press mixture evenly onto bottoms of 12 paper-lined baking cups.
- Soften gelatin in water in small saucepan; stir over low heat until dissolved.
- Beat cream cheese product, milk, sugar and almond extract in large mixing bowl at medium speed with electric mixer until well blended. Stir in gelatin. Pour into baking cups; freeze until firm.
- Place peaches in food processor or blender container; process until smooth. Spoon peach purée onto individual plates.
- Remove cheesecakes from freezer 10 minutes before serving. Peel off paper. Invert cheesecakes onto plates. Garnish with additional peach slices, raspberries and fresh mint leaves, if desired.

Makes 12 servings

Note: For a sweeter peach purée, add sugar to taste.

Nutrients per serving:

Calories	175	Cholesterol	11 mg
Fat	10 g	Sodium	180 mg

ORANGE TERRINE WITH STRAWBERRY SAUCE

1 package (3 ounces) ladyfingers, split
2 packages (4-serving size) *or* 1 package (8-serving size) JELL-O® Brand Orange Flavor Sugar Free Gelatin
1½ cups boiling water
1 cup orange juice
Ice cubes
1 tablespoon orange liqueur (optional)
2 teaspoons grated orange peel
3¼ cups (8 ounces) COOL WHIP® LITE® Whipped Topping, thawed, divided
1 package (10 ounces) BIRDS EYE® Strawberries in Syrup, thawed, puréed and strained

- Line bottom and sides of 9×5-inch loaf pan with plastic wrap. Line long sides of pan with ladyfingers so that they are vertical and their split sides face in.
- Dissolve gelatin in boiling water. Combine orange juice and ice cubes to make 1¾ cups. Add to gelatin, stirring until slightly thickened. Remove any unmelted ice. Stir in liqueur and orange peel.
- Gently stir in 2½ cups whipped topping. Spoon into prepared pan, trimming ladyfingers even with filling, if necessary. Arrange remaining ladyfingers on top of creamy mixture. Chill until firm, at least 3 hours.
- Unmold onto serving plate; remove plastic wrap. Cut into slices and serve on strawberry purée; garnish with remaining ¾ cup whipped topping. *Makes 12 servings*

Nutrients per serving:

Calories	100	Cholesterol	25 mg
Fat	3 g	Sodium	60 mg

CRANBERRY–APPLE ICE

1 can (12 ounces) frozen apple-cranberry juice concentrate, thawed
1½ cups MOTT'S® Chunky Apple Sauce
1 bottle (32 ounces) sugar-free lemon-lime flavored carbonated beverage (4 cups)

In 2-quart nonmetal bowl, combine all ingredients; mix well. Cover; freeze until firm. Scoop frozen mixture into 5-ounce drinking cups or spoon into dessert dishes.

Makes 14 servings, 7 cups

Nutrients per serving (½ cup):

Calories	33	Cholesterol	0 mg
Fat	0 g	Sodium	14 mg

ORANGE–APPLE ICE

1 jar (23 ounces) MOTT'S® Natural or Regular Apple Sauce
⅓ cup orange marmalade
3 egg whites, beaten stiff*

In medium bowl, combine apple sauce and marmalade; mix well. Carefully fold in beaten egg whites. Pour into 8- or 9-inch nonmetal square pan. Cover; freeze until firm. Scoop frozen mixture into dessert dishes or orange shells. *Makes 12 servings, 6 cups*

Tip: To make orange shells, use sharp knife to make sawtooth cut around middle of fruit, cutting inside to center only. Twist, pull apart and remove inside portion, scraping shells clean with spoon.

*Use only clean, uncracked eggs.

Nutrients per serving (½ cup):

Calories	51	Cholesterol	0 mg
Fat	0 g	Sodium	15 mg

APPLE–HONEYDEW ICE

2 cups sugar-free lemon-lime flavored carbonated beverage
1 cup MOTT'S® Regular Apple Sauce
1 small honeydew melon, seeded, rind removed, cut into chunks
⅛ teaspoon ground ginger
2 to 3 drops green food color (optional)

In food processor or blender, combine all ingredients; process until smooth. Pour into 8- or 9-inch nonmetal square pan. Cover; freeze until firm. Scoop frozen mixture into dessert dishes. *Makes 10 servings, 5 cups*

Nutrients per serving (½ cup):

Calories	37	Cholesterol	0 mg
Fat	0 g	Sodium	14 mg

Left to Right: Apple-Honeydew Ice, Orange-Apple Ice and Cranberry-Apple Ice

Cappuccino Bon Bons

CHOCOLATE BANANA POPS

2 cups cold skim milk
1 package (4-serving size) JELL-O® Chocolate Flavor Sugar Free Instant Pudding and Pie Filling
1 cup thawed COOL WHIP® LITE® Whipped Topping
½ cup mashed banana

- Pour milk into mixing bowl. Add pudding mix. Beat with wire whisk until well blended, 1 to 2 minutes. Gently stir in whipped topping and banana.
- Spoon about ⅓ cup into each of ten 5-ounce paper cups. Insert wooden spoon or stick or plastic spoon into each for handle. Freeze until firm, about 5 hours. To serve, press firmly on bottom of cup to release pop. *Makes 10 pops*

Nutrients per serving (1 pop):

Calories	60	Cholesterol	0 mg
Fat	1 g	Sodium	160 mg

CAPPUCCINO BON BONS

1 package DUNCAN HINES® Fudge Brownie Mix, Family Size
2 eggs
⅓ cup water
⅓ cup CRISCO® PURITAN® Oil
1½ tablespoons FOLGERS® Instant Coffee
1 teaspoon ground cinnamon
Whipped topping
Ground cinnamon or fresh fruit for garnish

1. Preheat oven to 350°F. Place 1½-inch foil cupcake liners on cookie sheet.
2. Combine brownie mix, eggs, water, oil, instant coffee and 1 teaspoon cinnamon. Stir with spoon until well blended, about 50 strokes. Fill each cupcake liner with 1 measuring tablespoon batter. Bake at 350°F for 12 to 15 minutes or until wooden toothpick inserted in center comes out clean. Cool completely. Garnish each bon bon with whipped topping and a dash of cinnamon or piece of fruit. Refrigerate until ready to serve. *Makes 40 bon bons*

Tip: To make larger bon bons, use 12 (2½-inch) foil cupcake liners and fill with ¼ cup batter. Bake for 28 to 30 minutes.

Nutrients per serving (1 bon bon):

Calories	87	Cholesterol	11 mg
Fat	4 g	Sodium	53 mg

EASY DARK CHERRY TART

1¾ cups QUAKER® Oats (quick or old fashioned, uncooked)
½ cup all-purpose flour
⅓ cup packed brown sugar
¼ teaspoon salt (optional)
⅓ cup (5⅓ tablespoons) margarine, melted
2 cans (16 ounces each) pitted dark sweet cherries, undrained
2 tablespoons granulated sugar
1 tablespoon cornstarch
½ teaspoon almond or vanilla extract

Heat oven to 350°F. Lightly oil 9-inch springform pan or pie plate. Combine oats, flour, brown sugar and salt. Add margarine; mix well. Reserve ⅓ cup for topping; press remaining mixture onto bottom and 1 inch up sides of prepared pan. Bake 15 minutes.

Drain cherries, reserving ⅓ cup liquid. In medium saucepan, combine granulated sugar and cornstarch. Gradually add reserved liquid, stirring until smooth. Add cherries and extract. Bring to a boil, stirring occasionally. Reduce heat; simmer about 1 minute or until thickened and clear, stirring constantly. Pour over baked crust. Sprinkle with reserved oat topping. Bake 15 to 18 minutes or until edges of crust are lightly browned. Store tightly covered in refrigerator. *Makes 10 servings*

Nutrients per serving:

Calories	235	Cholesterol	0 mg
Fat	7 g	Sodium	75 mg

Frozen Apple Sauce 'n' Fruit Cup

FROZEN APPLE SAUCE 'N' FRUIT CUP

1 can (11 ounces) mandarin orange segments, drained
1 package (10 ounces) frozen strawberries, thawed
1 cup MOTT'S® Chunky or Regular Apple Sauce
1 cup grapes, if desired
2 tablespoons orange juice concentrate

In medium bowl, combine all ingredients. Spoon fruit mixture into individual dishes or paper cups. Freeze until firm. Remove from freezer about 30 minutes before serving. Garnish if desired.

Makes 7 servings, 3½ cups

Nutrients per serving (½ cup):

Calories	107	Cholesterol	0 mg
Fat	0 g	Sodium	5 mg

CHOCOLATE CRACKLES

⅓ cup CRISCO® Shortening
1½ cups granulated sugar
1½ teaspoons vanilla
1 egg
2 egg whites
1⅔ cups all-purpose flour
½ cup unsweetened cocoa powder
1½ teaspoons baking powder
½ teaspoon salt (optional)
½ cup confectioners' sugar

1. Combine Crisco®, granulated sugar and vanilla in large bowl. Beat at medium speed of electric mixer until blended. Add egg and egg whites. Beat well. Stir in flour, cocoa, baking powder and salt. Cover and refrigerate at least 3 hours.
2. Heat oven to 350°F. Grease baking sheet lightly.
3. Place confectioners' sugar in shallow dish or large plastic food storage bag. Rub some confectioners' sugar lightly on fingers and palms of hands. Shape dough into 1-inch balls. Roll or shake in confectioners' sugar until coated. Place about 2 inches apart on baking sheet.
4. Bake 350°F for 7 to 8 minutes or until almost no indentation remains when touched lightly. *Do not overbake.* Cool on baking sheet 2 minutes. Remove to cooling rack.

Makes 4 dozen cookies

Nutrients per serving (2 cookies):

Calories	118	Cholesterol	9 mg
Fat	3 g	Sodium	29 mg

BLUEBERRY CRISP

3 cups cooked brown rice
3 cups fresh blueberries*
¼ cup plus 3 tablespoons firmly packed brown sugar, divided
Nonstick cooking spray
⅓ cup rice bran
¼ cup whole-wheat flour
¼ cup chopped walnuts
1 teaspoon ground cinnamon
3 tablespoons margarine

Combine rice, blueberries, and 3 tablespoons sugar. Coat 8 individual custard cups or 2-quart baking dish with nonstick cooking spray. Place rice mixture in cups or baking dish; set aside. Combine bran, flour, walnuts, remaining ¼ cup sugar, and cinnamon in bowl. Cut in margarine with pastry blender until mixture resembles coarse meal. Sprinkle over rice mixture. Bake at 375°F for 15 to 20 minutes or until thoroughly heated. Serve warm. *Makes 8 servings*

To Microwave: Prepare as directed using 2-quart microproof baking dish. Cook, uncovered, on HIGH 4 to 5 minutes, rotating dish once during cooking time. Let stand 5 minutes. Serve warm.

*Substitute frozen unsweetened blueberries for the fresh blueberries, if desired. Thaw and drain before using. Or, substitute your choice of fresh fruit or combinations of fruit for the blueberries, if desired.

Nutrients per serving:

Calories	243	Cholesterol	0 mg
Fat	8 g	Sodium	61 mg

Favorite recipe from **USA Rice Council**

Blueberry Crisp

TROPICAL BAR COOKIES

½ cup DOLE® Sliced Almonds, divided
1 cup all-purpose flour
⅓ cup margarine, melted
½ cup sugar, divided
1 can (20 ounces) DOLE® Crushed Pineapple in Syrup, drained
1 package (8 ounces) light cream cheese, softened
1 egg
1 teaspoon vanilla extract
⅓ cup flaked coconut

- Preheat oven to 350°F. Chop ¼ cup almonds for crust; mix with flour, margarine and ¼ cup sugar in medium bowl until crumbly. Press into bottom of 9-inch square pan. Bake 12 minutes.
- Beat pineapple, cream cheese, egg, remaining ¼ cup sugar and vanilla in large bowl until blended. Pour over crust. Top with coconut and remaining ¼ cup sliced almonds.
- Bake 35 to 40 minutes or until golden brown. Cool on wire rack. Refrigerate at least 2 hours before cutting into bars. *Makes 16 bars*

Nutrients per serving (1 cookie):

Calories	199	Cholesterol	28 mg
Fat	10 g	Sodium	111 mg

Spice Cake with Fresh Peach Sauce

SPICE CAKE WITH FRESH PEACH SAUCE

1 package DUNCAN HINES® Moist Deluxe Spice Cake Mix

Sauce
6 cups fresh sliced peaches
1 cup water
⅓ cup sugar
⅛ teaspoon ground cinnamon

1. Preheat oven to 350°F. Grease and flour 10-inch Bundt® or tube pan. Prepare, bake and cool cake following package directions for No-Cholesterol recipe. Dust with confectioners sugar, if desired.
2. For sauce, combine peaches and water in large saucepan. Cook over medium heat 5 minutes. Reduce heat. Cover and simmer 10 minutes. Cool. Reserve ½ cup peach slices. Combine remaining peaches with any cooking liquid, sugar and cinnamon in blender or food processor. Process until smooth. Stir in reserved peach slices. To serve, spoon peach sauce over cake slices.

Makes 12 to 16 servings

Tip: Fresh peach sauce can be served either warm or chilled.

Nutrients per serving:

Calories	299	Cholesterol	0 mg
Fat	10 g	Sodium	294 mg

PICNIC FRUIT TART

Crust

¾ cup flour
¼ cup oat bran
2 tablespoons sugar
¼ cup (½ stick) PARKAY® Margarine
2 to 3 tablespoons cold water

Filling

1 envelope unflavored gelatin
½ cup cold water
1 container (8 ounces) Light PHILADELPHIA BRAND® Pasteurized Process Cream Cheese Product, softened
¼ cup sugar *or* 6 packets sugar substitute
1 teaspoon grated lemon peel
¼ cup skim milk
⅓ cup KRAFT® Apricot Preserves
¾ cup grape halves
¾ cup plum slices

- Crust: Heat oven to 375°F.
- Mix flour, oat bran and 2 tablespoons sugar in medium bowl; cut in margarine until mixture resembles coarse crumbs. Sprinkle with 2 to 3 tablespoons water, mixing lightly with fork just until moistened. Roll into ball. Cover; refrigerate.
- On lightly floured surface, roll out dough to 11-inch circle. Place in 9-inch tart pan with removable bottom. Trim edges; prick bottom with fork.
- Bake 16 to 18 minutes or until golden brown; cool.
- Filling: Soften gelatin in ½ cup water in small saucepan; stir over low heat until dissolved. Cool.

Picnic Fruit Tart

- Beat cream cheese product, ¼ cup sugar and peel in large mixing bowl at medium speed with electric mixer until well blended. Gradually add gelatin and milk, mixing until well blended.
- Pour over crust. Refrigerate until firm.
- Heat preserves in small saucepan over low heat until thinned. Spread evenly over tart. Arrange fruit over preserves. Carefully remove rim of pan. *Makes 14 servings*

Prep time: 40 minutes plus refrigerating
Cook time: 18 minutes

Nutrients per serving:

Calories	150	Cholesterol	10 mg
Fat	6 g	Sodium	130 mg

Peach-Yogurt Pie with Almond Melba Sauce

PEACH–YOGURT PIE WITH ALMOND MELBA SAUCE

2 cups fresh, frozen or canned peaches
2 tablespoons granulated sugar
1 tablespoon almond-flavored liqueur
1 quart vanilla-flavored ice milk or frozen yogurt, softened
1 KEEBLER® READY-CRUST® Butter Flavored Pie Crust

Almond Melba Sauce
2 cups fresh or frozen raspberries
⅓ cup confectioners' sugar
2 tablespoons almond-flavored liqueur
1 tablespoon lemon juice
Light whipped topping, sliced peaches and raspberries for garnish (optional)

In blender or food processor, place peaches, granulated sugar and 1 tablespoon liqueur. (If using fresh peaches, add 1 teaspoon lemon juice.) Cover and blend until smooth. Fold peach purée into softened ice milk or yogurt. Spoon into pie crust and freeze until firm.

To prepare sauce, place raspberries, confectioners' sugar, 2 tablespoons liqueur and lemon juice in blender or food processor. Cover and process until smooth. Strain to remove seeds. Chill.

To serve, remove pie from freezer and let stand 5 minutes. Slice pie and top each serving with sauce, a dollop of whipped topping and additional peaches and raspberries, if desired.

Makes 8 servings

Nutrients per serving:

Calories	298	Cholesterol	9 mg
Fat	9 g	Sodium	203 mg

COCOA BROWNIES

4 egg whites
½ cup CRISCO® PURITAN® Oil
1 teaspoon vanilla
1⅓ cups granulated sugar
½ cup cocoa
1¼ cups all-purpose flour
¼ teaspoon salt
Confectioners' sugar (optional)

1. Heat oven to 350°F. Oil bottom of 9×9-inch pan. Set aside.
2. Place egg whites in large bowl. Beat with spoon until slightly frothy. Add Crisco® Puritan® Oil and vanilla. Mix thoroughly. Stir in granulated sugar and cocoa. Mix well. Stir in flour and salt until blended. Pour into pan.
3. Bake at 350°F for 26 to 28 minutes. *Do not overbake.* Cool completely before cutting. Sprinkle with confectioners' sugar, if desired.

Makes 1½ dozen brownies

Nutrients per serving (1 brownie):

Calories	150	Cholesterol	0 mg
Fat	7 g	Sodium	43 mg

CHOCOLATE CHIP COOKIES

2 cups all-purpose flour
1 teaspoon baking soda
½ teaspoon salt
1 egg
3 tablespoons water
1 teaspoon vanilla extract
1 cup firmly packed brown sugar
¼ cup CRISCO® PURITAN® Oil
½ cup semi-sweet chocolate chips

1. Heat oven to 375°F. Oil baking sheets well. Combine flour, baking soda and salt. Set aside. Combine egg, water and vanilla. Set aside.
2. Blend brown sugar and Crisco® Puritan® Oil in large bowl at low speed of electric mixer. Add egg mixture. Beat until smooth. Add flour mixture in three parts at lowest speed. Scrape bowl well after each addition. Stir in chocolate chips.
3. Drop dough by rounded teaspoonfuls onto baking sheets. Bake at 375°F for 7 to 8 minutes or until lightly browned. Cool on baking sheets 1 minute. Remove to wire racks.

Makes 3 dozen cookies

Nutrients per serving (1 cookie):

Calories	74	Cholesterol	6 mg
Fat	3 g	Sodium	57 mg

Top: Cocoa Brownies
Bottom: Chocolate Chip Cookies

LOVELY LEMON CHEESECAKE

1 whole graham cracker, crushed
1 package (4-serving size) JELL-O® Brand Sugar Free Lemon Flavor Gelatin
⅔ cup boiling water
1 cup 1% low-fat cottage cheese
1 container (8 ounces) light pasteurized process cream cheese product, softened
2 cups thawed COOL WHIP® LITE® Whipped Topping
1 cup reduced-calorie cherry pie filling

- Spray 8- or 9-inch springform pan or 9-inch pie plate with nonstick cooking spray. Sprinkle sides with half of graham cracker crumbs.
- Completely dissolve gelatin in boiling water in small bowl. Pour into blender container. Add cheeses; blend at medium speed, scraping down sides occasionally, about 2 minutes or until mixture is completely smooth. Pour into large bowl. Gently stir in whipped topping. Pour into prepared pan; smooth top. Sprinkle remaining crumbs around outside edge, leaving center plain. Chill until set, about 4 hours.
- Just before serving, decorate top of cheesecake with pie filling and cut.

Makes 8 servings

Nutrients per serving:

Calories	160	Cholesterol	15 mg
Fat	7 g	Sodium	330 mg

Lovely Lemon Cheesecake

APPLE–CINNAMON PECAN CAKE

2 cups all-purpose flour
2 teaspoons baking powder
1 teaspoon ground cinnamon
½ teaspoon ground nutmeg
½ cup margarine, softened
1 cup granulated sugar
2 eggs
1 teaspoon vanilla extract
⅔ cup *undiluted* CARNATION® Evaporated Lowfat Milk
3 cups peeled and finely diced or shredded baking apples (about 2 large)
¾ cup (3 ounces) chopped pecans
2 tablespoons powdered sugar

Preheat oven to 350°F. In medium bowl, combine flour, baking powder, cinnamon and nutmeg; set aside. In large mixer bowl, cream margarine and granulated sugar; beat in eggs and vanilla. With mixer at low speed, alternately add flour mixture and evaporated lowfat milk, ending with flour mixture. Stir in apples and pecans. Spread batter evenly into lightly greased 13×9-inch baking pan. Bake 40 to 45 minutes or until wooden pick inserted in center comes out clean. Cool 20 minutes. Sift powdered sugar over top. Cool completely before cutting.

Makes 24 servings

Note: Apples may be shredded by hand or in food processor.

Nutrients per serving:

Calories	155	Cholesterol	19 mg
Fat	7 g	Sodium	95 mg

ROYAL BANANA FRUIT SHORTCAKE

2 extra-ripe, medium DOLE® Bananas, peeled
1 package (18 ounces) yellow cake mix
Ingredients for cake mix
½ cup DOLE® Sliced Almonds
¾ cup DOLE® Pine-Orange-Guava Juice, divided
1 firm, medium DOLE® Banana, peeled
2 cups assorted sliced DOLE® Fresh Fruit
¼ cup semisweet chocolate chips
½ teaspoon margarine

- Place 2 extra-ripe bananas in blender. Process until puréed. Prepare cake according to package directions, using puréed bananas as part of the liquid measured with water.
- Spread batter in 2 greased 9-inch round cake pans. Sprinkle tops with almonds. Bake and cool as directed. Use one layer for recipe; freeze second layer for future use.
- Pour 3 tablespoons fruit juice onto large cake plate. Place cake on top to absorb liquid. Pour another 3 tablespoons juice over top of cake.
- Slice firm banana and combine with other fruits. Reserve 1 tablespoon fruit juice for chocolate sauce; pour remaining juice over fruit. Arrange fruit with juice over cake.
- Combine chocolate chips, 1 tablespoon reserved fruit juice and margarine in small microwave-safe bowl. Microwave on HIGH 10 to 30 seconds or until soft. Stir until smooth. Drizzle over fruit and cake. Refrigerate 30 minutes.

Makes 8 servings

Prep time: 15 minutes
Bake time: 30 minutes

Nutrients per serving:

Calories	208	Cholesterol	81 mg
Fat	7 g	Sodium	60 mg

Royal Banana Fruit Shortcake

ALL–AMERICAN PINEAPPLE & FRUIT TRIFLE

1 DOLE® Fresh Pineapple
1 cup frozen sliced peaches, thawed
1 cup frozen strawberries, thawed, sliced
1 cup frozen raspberries, thawed
1 angel food cake (10 inch)
1 package (4-serving size) instant sugar-free vanilla pudding mix
⅓ cup cream sherry
½ cup frozen whipped topping, thawed

- Twist crown from pineapple. Cut pineapple in half lengthwise. Refrigerate half for another use, such as fruit salad. Cut fruit from shell. Cut fruit into thin wedges. Reserve 3 wedges for garnish; combine remaining pineapple wedges with peaches, strawberries and raspberries.
- Cut cake in half. Freeze half for another use. Tear cake into chunks.
- Prepare pudding according to package directions.
- In 2-quart glass bowl, layer half of each: cake, sherry, fruit mixture and pudding. Repeat layer once. Cover; chill 1 hour or overnight.
- Just before serving, garnish with whipped topping and reserved pineapple wedges.

Makes 8 to 10 servings

Prep time: 20 minutes
Chill time: 1 hour

Nutrients per serving:

Calories	173	Cholesterol	4 mg
Fat	2 g	Sodium	129 mg

CHOCOLATE CAKE FINGERS

1 cup granulated sugar
1 cup all-purpose flour
⅓ cup HERSHEY'S® Cocoa
¾ teaspoon baking powder
¾ teaspoon baking soda
½ cup skim milk
¼ cup frozen egg substitute, thawed
¼ cup canola oil or vegetable oil
1 teaspoon vanilla extract
½ cup boiling water
Powdered sugar
1 teaspoon freshly grated orange peel
1½ cups frozen nondairy whipped topping, thawed
30 fresh strawberries or raspberries (optional)

Heat oven to 350°F. Line bottom of 13×9-inch baking pan with waxed paper. In large mixer bowl, stir together granulated sugar, flour, cocoa, baking powder and baking soda. Add milk, egg substitute, oil and vanilla; beat on medium speed of electric mixer 2 minutes. Add water, stirring with spoon until well blended. Pour batter into prepared pan.

Bake 16 to 18 minutes or until wooden toothpick inserted in center comes out clean. Place towel on wire rack; sprinkle with powdered sugar. Invert cake on towel; peel off waxed paper. Turn cake right side up. Cool completely. Cut cake into small rectangles (about 2¼×1¼ inches). Stir orange peel into whipped topping; spoon dollop on each piece of cake. Garnish with strawberry or raspberry, if desired.

Makes about 30 servings

Nutrients per serving:

Calories	80	Cholesterol	0 mg
Fat	3 g	Sodium	35 mg

Acknowledgments

FAVORITE BRAND NAME RECIPES MAGAZINE would like to thank the companies and organizations listed below for the use of their recipes in this magazine.

Armour Swift-Eckrich
Best Foods, a Division of CPC International Inc.
Black-Eyed Pea Jamboree—Athens, Texas
Borden Kitchens, Borden, Inc.
Carnation, Nestlé Food Company
Clear Springs Trout Company
The Creamette Company
The Dole Food Company
Florida Tomato Committee
The Fresh Garlic Association
Heinz U.S.A.
Hershey Chocolate U.S.A.
Keebler Company
Kellogg Company
Kraft General Foods, Inc.
Mott's U.S.A., A division of Cadbury Beverages Inc.
Nabisco Foods Company
National Broiler Council
National Live Stock and Meat Board
National Pasta Association
National Pork Producers Council
National Turkey Federation
Oscar Mayer Foods Corporation
Pace Foods, Inc.
The Procter & Gamble Company, Inc.
The Quaker Oats Company
Sargento Cheese Company, Inc.
StarKist Seafood Company
The Sugar Association, Inc.
Sunkist Growers, Inc.
The Times-Picayune
USA Rice Council
Wisconsin Milk Marketing Board

Photo Credits

FAVORITE BRAND NAME RECIPES MAGAZINE would like to thank the companies and organizations listed below for the use of their photographs in this magazine.

Borden Kitchens, Borden, Inc.
Clear Springs Trout Company
The Dole Food Company
Keebler Company
Kellogg Company
Kraft General Foods, Inc.
Mott's U.S.A., A division of Cadbury Beverages Inc.
National Broiler Council
National Live Stock and Meat Board
National Pork Producers Council
National Turkey Federation
Pace Foods, Inc.
The Procter & Gamble Company, Inc.
Sargento Cheese Company, Inc.
StarKist Seafood Company
The Sugar Association, Inc.
USA Rice Council

Index

METRIC CONVERSION CHART

VOLUME MEASUREMENT*

1/8 teaspoon = 0.5 mL
1/4 teaspoon = 1 mL
1/3 teaspoon = 1 mL
1/2 teaspoon = 2 mL
3/4 teaspoon = 4 mL
1 teaspoon = 5 mL
½ tablespoon = 7 mL
1 tablespoon = 15 mL
1½ tablespoons = 22 mL
2 tablespoons = 25 mL
3 tablespoons = 45 mL
1/4 cup = 50 mL
1/3 cup = 80 mL
1/2 cup = 125 mL
2/3 cup = 160 mL
3/4 cup = 180 mL
1 cup = 250 mL (236.58)
1½ cups = 375 mL
2 cups = 1 pt. = 500 mL
2½ cups = 625 mL
3 cups = 750 mL
3½ cups = 825 mL
4 cups = 1 qt. = 1 L
1 fluid ounce (2 Tbs.) = 30 mL
4 fluid ounces (½ cup) = 125 mL
8 fluid ounces (1 cup) = 250 mL
12 fluid ounces (1½ cups) = 375 mL
16 fluid ounces (2 cups) = 500 mL
(including fluid ounces)

WEIGHT (MASS)*

½ ounce = 15 g
1 ounce = 30 g (28.35)
2 ounces = 60 g
3 ounces = 85 g
4 ounces = 115 g
8 ounces = 225 g
12 ounces = 340 g
16 ounces = 1 lb. = 450 g
2 pounds = 900 g
**Ounces to Grams*

BAKING PAN SIZES

Utensil	Metric Volume	Metric Measure in cm	Closest Size in Inches or Volume
Baking or	2 L	20 x 5	8 x 2
Cake Pan	2.5 L	22 x 5	9 x 2
	3 L	30 x 20 x 5	12 x 8 x 2
	3.5 L	33 x 23 x 5	13 x 9 x 2
Loaf Pan	1.5 L	20 x 10 x 7	8 x 4 x 3
	2 L	23 x 13 x 7	9 x 5 x 3
Round Layer	1.2 L	20 x 4	8 x 1½
Cake Pan	1.5 L	23 x 4	9 x 1½
Pie Pan	750 mL	20 x 3	8 x 1¼
	1 L	23 x 3	9 x 1¼
Baking Dish	1 L		1 qt.
or Casserole	1.5 L		1½ qt.
	2 L		2 qt.

DIMENSION

1/16 inch = 2 mm
1/8 inch= 0.5 cm
3/16 inch = 0.5 cm
1/4 inch = 0.5 cm
3/8 inch = 1 cm
1/2 inch = 1.5 cm
5/8 inch = 1.5 cm
3/4 inch = 2 cm
1 inch = 2.5 cm (2.54)
1½ inches = 4 cm
2 inches = 5 cm

OVEN TEMPERATURES

250° F = 120° C
275° F = 140° C
300° F = 150° C
325° F = 160° C
350° F = 180° C
375° F = 190° C
400° F = 200° C
425° F = 220° C
450° F = 230° C
**(– 32 x 5 ÷ 9) (low temps. do exact conversion)*